Lincoln
on
Lincoln

Lincoln
on
Lincoln

Selected and Edited
by
Paul M. Zall

THE UNIVERSITY PRESS OF KENTUCKY

Publication of this volume was made possible in part by a grant
from the National Endowment for the Humanities.

Scholarly publisher for the Commonwealth,
serving Bellarmine College, Berea College, Centre
College of Kentucky, Eastern Kentucky University,
The Filson Club Historical Society, Georgetown College,
Kentucky Historical Society, Kentucky State University,
Morehead State University, Murray State University,
Northern Kentucky University, Transylvania University,
University of Kentucky, University of Louisville,
and Western Kentucky University.

Editorial and Sales Offices: The University Press of Kentucky
663 South Limestone Street, Lexington, Kentucky 40508-4008

03 02 01 00 99   5 4 3 2 1

Library of Congress Cataloging-in-Publication Data

Lincoln, Abraham, 1809-1865.
   Lincoln on Lincoln / selected & edited by Paul M. Zall.
      p.   cm.
   Includes biblioraphical references and index.
   ISBN 0-8131-2141-8 (alk. paper)
   1. Lincoln, Abraham, 1809-1865. 2. Presidents—United States Biography.
   3. Lincoln, Abraham, 1809-1865—Psychology. I. Zall, Paul M. II. Title.
   E457.L7375   1999
   973.7'092—dc21
   [B]   99-15217

FOR LEE ZALL

CONTENTS

PREFACE

The excerpts in this book have been selected to tell a story of Abraham Lincoln's life in his own words. They have been put together from his writings, speeches, and interviews with preference for those recorded as the events or ideas unfolded. His own writings have been supplemented by reports from newspapers and reliable witnesses, with all sources listed in an appendix.

Primary resources were holdings in the Library of Congress and the Henry E. Huntington Library with its Judd Stewart collection of three thousand books and manuscripts by and about Lincoln along with the nine thousand volumes on the Civil War collected by J.P. Nicholson.

In the course of this work, three of my greatest resources have died—Don Fehrenbacher, Robert Gray Gunderson, and Helene Wickham Koon. Their loss diminishes the joy of finishing. But I owe a deep debt of gratitude for aid and comfort to the Technical Services staff of the Huntington Library, not least rare-book cataloger Elisabeth Zall, to Warren Johnson for processing the words, and to my old friend Thomas F. Schwartz and the Abraham Lincoln Association for permission to reprint from the *Collected Works* when original texts were wanting.

SOME IMPORTANT DATES

1809 February   Born about 3 miles south of Hodgenville, Ky.

1816 December   Family moves near Pigeon Creek, Ind.

1818 October   Nancy Hanks Lincoln dies from tremetol poisoning

1819 December   Father rejoins children after several months in Kentucky to wed Sarah Bush Johnston

1828 January   Sister Sally dies in childbirth, aged 21

      April   Takes first flatboat voyage to New Orleans

1830 March   Family moves ten miles south of Decatur, Ill.

1831 March   Leaves home to seek his fortune; hires on for another flatboat trip to New Orleans; returns to settle as clerk in New Salem, Ill.

1832   Elected captain in Black Hawk war, serves 4 months; unsuccessful candidate for legislature

1833 January   Partner in grocery

      May   Postmaster

1834   Named deputy surveyor

      August   Elected to Assembly in Vandalia

      December   Attends legislature at $4 a day while in session

---

Some Important Dates

1835	August	Death of Ann Rutledge supposedly causes depression
1836	September	Licensed to practice law
1837	April	Moves to new capital, Springfield; law partner with John Todd Stuart
1839		Practices on new 8th Judicial Circuit (until named president)
1841	January	Broken engagement to Mary Todd supposedly causes depression
	Summer	Seeks relief with best friend Joshua Speed at Louisville
1842	November	Weds Mary Todd
1843	August	Robert Todd Lincoln born
1844	Autumn	Visit to boyhood home evokes poems
1846	March	Son Edward born
1847	December	Sits in 30th Congress, Washington
1848	September	With family, tours New England for Whig party
1850	February	Son Edward dies of pulmonary tuberculosis
	December	Son William "Willie" born
1851	January	Father dies at age seventy-two
1853	April	Son Thomas "Tad" born.
1856	May	Aids in forming Republican party in Illinois
1858	August–October	Debates Stephen A. Douglas in race for U.S. Senate; wins popular vote, loses in legislature that named Senators
1859	December	Sends autobiographical sketch back East for press
1860	May	Made Republican nominee
	6 November	Elected president
1861	March	Inaugurated 16th president
	April	Fort Sumter attacked

Some Important Dates

1862	February	Son William dies in White House of bronchial pneumonia
	September	Circulates preliminary Emancipation Proclamation, to be effective 1 January 1863
1863	July	Crucial victories at Vicksburg and Gettysburg.
	November	Gettysburg Address
1864	June	Nominated for second term as National Union candidate.
	November	Re-elected by popular and overwhelming electoral vote
1865	February	Lobbies 13th Amendment through Congress
	March	Second inaugural address offers "charity for all"
	April	Lee surrenders on 9th; Booth kills Lincoln, who dies at 7:22 A.M., 15 April

Note: For a complete chronology, see Miers, *Lincoln Day by Day*.

INTRODUCTION

This book came about in trying to understand what Lincoln was really like. He leads in every twentieth-century poll of presidential greatness. He is perennially subjected to biographies for all ages. Yet his personality remains one of the nation's unsolved mysteries. He himself composed two biographical sketches to be used for the 1860 presidential campaign, so with these as matrix I have interwoven extracts from correspondence, speeches, interviews, and reliable reports to provide a tapestry of his life in his own words.

He was not the kind of person to bare his soul in public or in private. "Even, between ourselves," lamented Mary Todd Lincoln, "when our deep and touching sorrows, were *one* and the same, his expressions were few."[1] Yet to sensitive readers even those few expressions could open a view on the inner struggle to reconcile personal ambition and civic virtue, conscience and Constitution, ultimately the will of God and the will of the people. I take this struggle to be the source of moral force that cemented a nation divided and that sustains some of us even now.

The story unfolding in his own words is in no way a conventional confessional autobiography. Absent is such a celebrated episode as Lincoln's star-crossed love for Ann Rutledge—simply because he himself never mentioned it. But concise linking notes may serve to add such details when needed for context or clarification. This is especially

1

so respecting the means he used to make something out of nothing and the influence of mentors as he made his way in the world. Sometimes silent on such vital matters, he nevertheless reveals means and ends between the lines as the linking notes are designed to do between excerpts.

In the context of his contemporary world, Lincoln could be seen as the New Man for a New Age, a poster boy for what we now know as the industrial middle class rising from the steaming expansion of the 1840s and 1850s. Half his life was spent in Springfield, Illinois, a way station for transients moving westward and capital of the state when iron and oil discoveries energized a transport system that enabled him to rise as one of the region's leading railroad lawyers.

At the same time, an expanding information technology offered new media for reaching an unprecedented reading class. This was a generation of newspaper readers. Their newspapers, much larger than our own in size if not weight, carried little news but much information for an upwardly mobile nation. Readers eagerly sought instant culture, supplied by the press in reprints of plays, entire novels, Congressional debates, along with techniques for transforming farmers to factory foremen and more. The way to wealth was paved in newsprint: almost four hundred dailies, three thousand weeklies, and, by 1860, services of the Associated Press exploiting a spreading telegraph system. By 1860 literacy rate among soldiers on both sides hovered around 80 percent.

This communication revolution helps to explain Lincoln's reliance on newspapers for education and, later, reformation of a nation. Newspapers supplied his early schooling when books were scarce. As postmaster he had access to national along with regional press. As campaigner he compiled a notebook of clippings to show his views on slavery. As author, he published one book, and that consisted of press reports of the debates with Stephen A. Douglas. And as President he preferred the Associated Press transcription to his own script of the Gettysburg Address. Given his symbiotic relation with the press, I have given newspaper reports and interviews equal space with his correspondence. We know that he had the chance to review and revise his speeches reported in the *Congressional Globe,* prototype of the *Congressional Record,* and that he would distribute drafts of other documents for friends to review and revise. Such drafts have added value in allowing us to see Lincoln's mind in motion as, for instance, he reworks suggestions for the first inaugural address, or works through the second inaugural address seemingly on his own. Measuring the authenticity of his words as recollected by others has been made much easier thanks to the eponymous book by Don and Virginia Fehrenbacher noted below. I have used quotation marks to distinguish recollections of others; otherwise, this is Lincoln's own story told in his own way in his own words.

Extracting excerpts, of course, weakens the integrity of Lincoln's documents, but I have tried to retain the integrity of his style. To have indicated omissions (. . .) would have resulted in polka dotted pages, so ellipses were used sparingly and then only to show major omissions. I have not reproduced such quirks as using dashes in place of periods, but do respect Lincoln's use of commas to show pauses and pacing in reading aloud—as his writings were meant to be read. I have retained misspelling and grammatical errors in order to show how they diminished over the years—except in drafts written under influence of powerful feelings.

Editorial apparatus is streamlined so that focus stays narrowed to Lincoln's events or ideas rather than the editor's.

Because excerpts come from a variety of sources, incongruity runs rampant—as when the Fell sketch uses the first person pronoun "I" while the Scripps sketch uses "he" and even "A." But this is the traditional mode followed by Tristram Shandy in the history of his own life. His Book 9, Chapter 25, lays out the rule: "Let people tell their stories their own way."

ABBREVIATIONS

CW	Basler et al., *Collected Works of Abraham Lincoln*
F	Fell, vol. 3 of *CW*
F2	Fehrenbacher and Fehrenbacher, *Recollected Words of Abraham Lincoln*
Facs	facsimile
LH	*Lincoln Herald*
S	Scripps, vol. 4 of *CW*
MTL	Turner and Turner, Mary Todd Lincoln's letters
W&D	Wilson and Davis, *Lincoln's Informants*

Other manuscripts are listed with Huntington accession numbers, usually prefixed by HM or LN, or with frame numbers of Library of Congress film by the Reference Division there. See bibliography for complete publication information on the above sources.

1

SURVIVING THE FRONTIER

1809–1830

I was born February 12, 1809 in Hardin County, Kentucky.[1]
My parents were both born in Virginia, of undistinguished
families—second families, perhaps I should say. My pater-
nal grandfather, Abraham Lincoln, emigrated from
Rockingham County, Virginia, to Kentucky, about 1781 or
2, where, a year or two later, he was killed by indians, not
in battle, but by stealth, when he was laboring to open a
farm in the forest.

The story of his death, and of Uncle Mordecai killing
one of the Indians, is the legend more strongly than others imprinted upon my mind and memory.[2]

> Two young sons, Mordecai and younger brother Thomas,
> who would one day father the president, were with
> Grandfather Lincoln when he was shot, May 1786, on the
> 400-acre site he had helped to survey in Jefferson County
> (*Register Kentucky State Historical Society* 27 [1929] 408).
> Robert Todd Lincoln gave legendary details of the killing,
> telling how fifteen-year-old Mordecai ran to a neighbor-
> ing cabin, seized his rifle, and shot the culprit carrying
> off little Thomas. Robert Lincoln then added that, since
> Grandfather had left no will, his entire estate, consisting

of two other 400-acre warrants as well, went to an eldest son, leaving Thomas penniless (Angle, *Portrait*, 59).

Thomas, the youngest son, and father of the present subject, by the early death of his father, and very narrow circumstances of his mother, even in childhood was a wandering laboring boy, and grew up litterally without education. He never did more in the way of writing than to bunglingly sign his own name,[3] which I suppose is the reason why I know so little of our family history.[4]

Before he was grown, he passed one year as a hired hand with his uncle Isaac on Wataga, a branch of the Holsteen River.[5] Getting back into Kentucky, and having reached his 28th year, he married Nancy Hanks—mother of the present subject—in the year 1806. She also was born in Virginia.

The present subject has no brother or sister of the whole or half blood. He had a sister, older than himself, who was grown and married, but died many years ago, leaving no child. Also a brother, younger than himself, who died in infancy.

> Baby Thomas died in 1812. Sister Sarah, or Sally, two years older than Abraham, died in childbirth, January 1828.

Before leaving Kentucky he and his sister were sent for short periods, to A.B.C. schools, the first kept by Zacharia Riney, and the second by Caleb Hazel.

> Riney, a local farmer, and Hazel, the tavern keeper, taught the ABCs; reading was delayed until age 6, writing to age 8. Parents paid per session. Learning was by rote memory and aloud (thus "blab schools") (McVey 64-66; McClure

87, 213; E.J. Monaghan, *A Common Heritage* [Hamden, Conn.: Archon Press, 1983], 32-33).

At this time his father resided on Knob-creek, on the road from Bardstown Ky. to Nashville Tenn. at a point three, or three and a half miles South or South-West of Atherton's ferry on the Rolling Fork. (I was born on Nolin, very much nearer Hodgin's-Mill than the Knob Creek place is. My earliest recollection, however, is of the Knob Creek place.)[6]

"I remember that old home very well! Our farm was composed of three fields. It lay in the valley surrounded by high hills and deep gorges. Sometimes when there came a big rain in the hills the water would come down through the gorges and spread all over the farm. The last thing that I remember of doing there was one Saturday afternoon. The other boys planted the corn in what we called the big field—it contained seven acres—and I dropped the pumpkin seeds. I dropped two seeds every other hill and every other row. The next Sunday morning there came a big rain in the hills. It did not rain a drop in the valley, but the water coming down through the gorges washed ground, corn, pumpkin seeds and all clear off the field."[7]

From this place he removed to what is now Spencer county Indiana, in the Autumn of 1816. This removal was partly on account of slavery; but chiefly on account of the difficulty in land titles in Ky.[8]

After five years farming the place, Thomas Lincoln learned that his deed was defective because of faulty state records. The mention of slavery was a late addition in the manuscript, but the family's church had split up over the issue and Thomas Lincoln made a two-week tour seeking a homesite in Indiana several months after the state had drafted a new constitution that outlawed slavery in spring of 1816 (Warren 12-14, 16). The land-claim problem must have taken precedence. Thomas Lincoln had already lost more than $200 and 500-plus acres at Mill Creek and Sinking Springs because of faulty recordkeeping. Now a Philadelphian claimed 1,000 acres being farmed by Lincoln and nine other families.

DECEMBER 1816

We reached our new home about the time the State came into the Union. It was a wild region, with many bears and other wild animals still in the woods[9]. . . an unbroken forest.

Indiana came into the Union December 1816.

Lincoln would later say he never passed a harder experience than that journey. The family covered 90 miles in about five days by horse, foot, and ferry across the Ohio—probably to the mouth of Anderson River. They then trekked through forests of oak, hickory, and hazel and brush so thick "a man could scarcely get through on foot" (Raymond 6-7; Warren 20; W&D 217).

The clearing away of surplus wood was the great task a head. A. though very young, was large for his age, and had an axe put into his hands at once; and from that till within his twentythird year, he was almost constantly handling that most useful instrument—less, of course, in plowing and harvesting seasons.

FEBRUARY 1817

At this place A. took an early start as a hunter, which was never much improved afterwards. A few days before the completion of his eigth year, in the absence of his father, a flock of wild turkeys approached the new log-cabin, and A. with a rifle gun, standing inside, shot through a crack, and killed one of them. He has never since pulled a trigger on any larger game.

> Lincoln's hunting prowess seems diminished by reports that a local salt lick attracted flocks of turkeys numbering fifty to seventy-five, so heedless they would walk directly up to the muzzle of a gun (Cockrum 437).

1818–1819

In his tenth year he was kicked by a horse, and apparently killed for a time.

> William Herndon's biography makes light of the concussion suffered when kicked by a mill horse, yet the boy lay unconscious overnight, suggesting a serious injury. More serious still was a "milksick" epidemic that killed his mother along with her aunt and uncle; she died 5 October of tremetol poisoning from milk of cows that had consumed white snakeroot (*Eupatorium urtica-folium*) (Jordan 105-10; Warren 51-53; Angle, *Herndon's,* 51).

In the autumn of 1818 his mother died; and a year afterwards his father married Mrs. Sally Johnston, at Elizabeth-Town, Ky—a widow, with three children of her first marriage.

> Thomas Lincoln left ten-year-old Abraham and twelve-year-old Sally alone on the frontier for nine months while he courted Sally Bush Johnston, sister of a friend and widow of the county jailer. They were married at Elizabethtown by Methodist preacher George L. Rogers on

December 2, but she would not leave Kentucky until satisfying all debts. Her own children were Elizabeth, nine, John, seven, and Matilda (Tildy), five (Herndon and Weik 1:22-24; Warren 62-64).

1819–1824

A. went to A.B.C. schools by little, kept successively by Andrew Crawford, —— Sweeney, and Azel W. Dorsey . . . now thinks that the agregate of all his schooling did not amount to one year.[10]

Located about a mile and a half from the Lincoln homestead, the school at Little Pigeon Creek charged tuition of a dollar or two per session, lasting a month or less when the children could be spared from labor. One contemporary recollected the Lincolns dropping out because their father could not afford the steep fees (Rice 458). In school they studied Dilworth's speller, which included Aesop's fables, and Lincoln went on to study arithmetic. Schoolmaster Dorsey recalled Abraham owning a battered old arithmetic Thomas Lincoln had found somewhere (Raymond 21). Dorsey, a farmer, and his guardian James Swaney (not Sweeney) along with Justice-of-the-Peace Crawford taught reading, writing and ciphering "to the rule of three"; i.e., solving for a fourth term when three are known. But at least a quarter of the exercises in Lincoln's notebook (*CW* l: preliminary pages) derived from Dilworth's *Schoolmaster's Assistant*, reprinted as late as the 1790s, which could fit the description Dorsey offers (Dorfman 63). It seems only spelling was tested. This would be by open spelling bee, a lively social event for the whole neighborhood (McVey 64-65). Sally Bush Johnston Lincoln insisted that Thomas had encouraged the boy to read, even taking on extra work rather than interrupt reading (W&D 107). But books were very expensive. The Parson Weems volumes often cited would have cost the equivalent of $30 in today's terms; the copy of Ramsay's *Life of Washington* he is supposed to have ruined in the rain would have cost three times that! (Mearns, *Three*, 50-52).

If a straggler supposed to understand latin, happened to sojourn in the neighborhood, he was looked upon as a wizzard. There was absolutely nothing to excite ambition for education. Of course when I came of age I did not know much. Still somehow, I could read, write, and cipher to the Rule of Three; but that was all.[11]

The earliest days of my being able to read, I got hold of a small book, Weems' "Life of Washington." I remember all the accounts there given of the battlefields and struggles for the liberties of the country, and none fixed themselves upon my imagination so deeply as the struggle at Trenton, New Jersey. The crossing of the river; the contest with the Hessians; the great hardships endured at that time; all fixed themselves on my memory more than any single revolutionary event. I recollect thinking then, boy even though I was, that there must have been something more than common that those men struggled for.[12]

> "Washington and his little *forlorn hope,* pressed on through the darksome night, pelted by an incessant storm of hail and snow. On approaching the river, nine miles above Trenton, they heard the unwelcome roar of ice, loud crashing along the angry flood. But the object before them was too *vast* to allow one thought about difficulties" (Cunliffe 83).

He was never in a college or Academy as a student; and never inside of a college or accademy building till since he had a law-license. What he has in the way of education, he has picked up. After he was twenty-three, and had separated from his father, he studied English grammar, imperfectly of course, but so as to speak and write as well as he now does. He studied and nearly mastered the Six-books of Euclid, since he was a member of Congress. He regrets his want of education, and does what he can to supply the want.[13]

> Opening of a post office a mile and a half away gave Lincoln access to newspapers from across the Ohio Valley, where the number of papers, mostly weeklies, rose from 79 in 1820 to 354 in 1850. Yearly subscriptions cost about $2.50, when wages for splitting logs came to about 25 cents a hundred. The press carried cultural as well as agricultural and political information—Indiana's first newspaper introduced itself with an Oliver Goldsmith essay as promise of literature to come (Venable 194-95; Rusk 1:156-57). Newspapers also carried complete public documents with Congressional debates, invaluable for someone of Lincoln's interests. Neighbors recalled that his first speech was at a debating club ("did pretty well") and that he "used to walk 6 miles" to another debating club where "men of no education whatever" would practice what they called "polemics" (Howard 393; Mearns, *Lincoln Papers,* 1:157-58).
>
> Some neighbors owned a surprisingly rich collection of books, among them Hugh Blair's *Lectures on Rhetoric,* James Thomson's *Seasons,* Machiavelli's *Art of War* and Cervantes' *Don Quixote.* (Hickey 202). The "New Salem Literary Society," meeting in James Rutledge's tavern, could supply another twenty-five books, while newspa-

pers provided grist for such debate topics as "Should Congress reduce the price of public land" or "Should females be educated?" (Pond 6-17). Contemporaries say Lincoln about 1827 published newspaper essays, since disappeared, supposedly on debate topics such as the Constitution and alcoholism (Warren 169-70).

1826–1827

"I constructed a little flatboat, large enough to take a barrel or two of things, that we had gathered, with myself and little bundle, down to New Orleans. A steamer was coming down the river. We have, you know, no wharves on the Western streams; and the custom was, if passengers were at any of the landings, for them to go out in a boat, the steamer stopping and taking them on board.

"Two men came down to the shore in carriages with trunks, and looking at the different boats singled out mine, and asked, 'Who owns this?' I answered, 'I do.' 'Will you,' said one of them, 'take us and our trunks out to the steamer?' 'Certainly,' said I. I was very glad to have the chance of earning something. I supposed that each of them would give me two or three bits. I sculled them out to the steamboat.

"They got on board, and I lifted up their heavy trunks, and put them on deck. The steamer was about to put on steam again, when I called out that they had forgotten to pay me. Each of them took from his pocket a silver half-dollar, and threw it on the floor of my boat. I could scarcely credit that I, a poor boy, had earned a dollar in less than a day—that by honest work I had earned a dollar. The world seemed wider and fairer before me. I was a more hopeful and confident being from that time."[14]

By contrast, his wages for a flatboat trip to New Orleans the next year would be $8 a month (Howard 390-91; Warren 177). Often Lincoln would take wages for rail-splitting and the like in socks, jeans, etc., or 25 cents a day and board (W&D 660).

"With few mechanics and but little means in the West, we used to make our shoes last a great while with much mending, and sometimes, when far gone, we found the leather so rotten the stitches would not hold.[15]

"You know the nature of buckskin when wet and dried by the sun they would shrink and mine kept shrinking until they left for several inches of my legs bare between the top of my Socks and the lower part of my breeches and whilst I was growing taller, they were becoming shorter and so much tighter that they left a blue streak around my leg which you can see to this day."[16]

1828

When he was nineteen, still residing in Indiana, he made his first trip upon a flat-boat to New-Orleans. He was a hired hand merely; and he and a son of the owner, without other assistance, made the trip. The nature of part of the cargo-load, as it was called—made it necessary for them to linger and trade along the Sugar coast—and one night they were attacked by seven negroes with intent to kill and rob them. They were hurt some in the melee, but succeeded in driving the negroes from the boat, and then "cut cable" and left.

With Allen Gentry he made the trip in about three months, returning by steamboat in three weeks. Their cargo of meat, corn, and flour was exchanged for sugar and similar produce. Armed only with clubs, they routed the attackers by pretending to have weapons: "Lincoln get the guns and Shoot!" (W&D 131).

1 MARCH 1830

A. having just completed his 21st year, his father and family, with the families of the two daughters and sons-in-law, of his step-mother, left the old homestead in Indiana, and came to Illinois.

> The stepmother could not bear to lose her daughters heading west for their own lands, but the family also feared the epidemic of "milk-sick" that had this year so far taken four cows and eleven calves (Warren 204-6, 208, 266 n. 14; Richmond 51). Before leaving, they sold enough property to acquire $500 for relocating in the fabled fertile soil of Illinois.

Their mode of conveyance was waggons driven by ox-teams and A. drove one of the teams.[17]

"I was afoot but not barefoot. In my young days I frequently went barefooted but on that occasion I had on a substantial pair of shoes—it was a cold day in March and I never went barefooted in cold weather. I will remember that trip as long as I live. I crossed the Wabash at Vincennes and the river being high the road on the low prairie was covered with water a half mile at a stretch and the water covered with ice—the only means by which I could keep the road was by observing the stakes placed as guides when the water is over the road."[18]

> They left Vincennes, crossed the Wabash the second day, went through Palestine, Greenup, Paradise, and finally reached Decatur (*Lincoln Way* 18-19, 22). With thirteen

people, five under age eight, the family made the 225-mile journey in three covered wagons drawn by two oxen and a horse (Warren 204-6).

They reached the county of Macon, and stopped there some time within the month of March. His father and family settled a new place on the North side of the Sangamon river, at the junction of the timber-land and prairie, about ten miles Westerly from Decatur. Here they built a log-cabin, into which they removed, and made sufficient of rails to fence ten acres of ground, fenced and broke the ground, and raised a crop of sow corn upon it the same year. These are, or are supposed to be, the rails about which so much is being made just now, though they are far from being the first, or only rails ever made by A.

> The allusion to "rails" jests about the campaign to popularize him as the "railsplitter," initiated by his cousin's marching down the aisle at the state convention nominating Lincoln their candidate for president. Cousin John Hanks carried a rail on his shoulders alleging it had been split by Lincoln as a youth. Hanks subsequently made a living selling pieces of such pseudorelics, for rails became a popular symbol in the campaign for "The Rail Lincoln." He had indeed split rails, for cousin Nancy Hanks Miller recalled bartering "one yard of brown jeans (richly died with walnut bark) for every four hundred rails made, until he should have enough for a pair of trowsers," and others estimated he split a thousand rails (Howells, *Life*, 24n).

The sons-in-law were temporarily settled at other places in the county. In the autumn all hands were greatly afflicted with augue and fever, to which they had not been used, and by which they were greatly discouraged—so much so that they determined on leaving the county. They remained however, through the succeeding winter, which was the winter of the celebrated "deep snow" of Illinois.

> The family's cure for ague and fever consisted of "barks," Peruvian bark and whiskey. Local lore says the great snow was so high, a farmer could pick corn extending through the drifts. Lincoln himself caught a cold and was laid up for three weeks—at the Warnick home, where he recuperated by reading Warnick's law books (Richmond 59).

During that winter, A. together with his step-mother's son, John D. Johnston, and John Hanks, yet residing in Macon county, hired themselves to one Denton Offutt, to take a flat boat from Beardstown Illinois to New-Orleans; and for that purpose, were to join him—Offut—at Springfield, Ill. so soon as the snow should go off. When it did go off which was about the 1st of March 1831, the county was so flooded, as to make traveling by land impracticable; to obviate which difficulty they purchased a large canoe and came down the Sangamon river in it. This is the time and manner of A's first entrance into Sangamon County.[19]

2

FINDING A NEW LIFE
IN NEW SALEM

1831–1837

An adventurer from Kentucky, Denton Offutt promised cousin John Hanks, stepbrother John Johnston, and Lincoln 50 cents a day and 60 dollars to trade a flat-boat load of pork, corn, and live hogs down to New Orleans. Offutt came from a respected Kentucky family but somehow had acquired a reputation as inept and shifty ("always had his eyes open to the main chance") (Thomas, *New Salem*, 43).

APRIL 1831

They found Offutt at Springfield, but learned from him that he had failed in getting a boat at Beardstown. This lead to their hiring themselves to him at $12 per month, each; and getting the timber out of the trees and building a boat at old Sangamon Town on the Sangamon river, seven miles N.W. of Springfield[1] . . . [They] finished and took her out in the course of the spring.

The time at which we crossed the mill dam, being in the last days of April, the water was lower than it had been since the breaking of winter in February, or than it was for several weeks after. The principal difficulties we encountered in descending the river, were from the drifted timber, which obstructions all know is not difficult to be removed.[2]

> At the Sangamon Town sawmill on Prairie Creek they cut timber on government land nearby, spent about four weeks making the boat, and reached the New Salem mill dam about 19 April (Howells, *Life*, 27). When the boat grounded on the dam, Lincoln bored a hole in the overhanging end trying to free it.

It was in connection with this boat that occurred the ludicrous incident of sewing up the hogs eyes. Offutt bought thirty-odd large fat live hogs, but found difficulty in driving them from where purchased to the boat, and thereupon conceived the whim that he could sew up their eyes and drive them where he pleased. No sooner thought of than decided, he put his hands, including A. at the job, which they completed—all but the driving. In their blind condition they could not be driven out of the lot or field they were in. This expedient failing, they were tied and hauled on carts to the boat.

JULY 1831

A's father, with his own family and others mentioned, had, in pursuance of their intention, removed from Macon to Coles county. John D. Johnston, the stepmother's son, went to them; and A. stopped indefinitely, and, for the first time, as it were, by himself at New-Salem, before-mentioned. This was in July 1831.

SEPTEMBER 1831

During this boat enterprize acquaintance with Offutt, who was previously an entire stranger, he conceved a liking for A. and believing he could turn him to account, he contracted with him to act as clerk for him, on his return from New-Orleans, in charge of a store and Mill at New-Salem.

Offutt rented the mill at the dam and left Lincoln in charge of the goods in September. His assistant clerk said Lincoln and he "slept on the same cot, and when one turned over the other had to do likewise" (W&D 17; Howells, *Life*, 28).

APRIL 1832

In less than a year Offutt's business was failing—had almost failed—when the Black-Hawk war of 1832 broke out. A. joined a volunteer company, and to his own surprize, was elected captain of it. He says he has not since had any success in life which gave him so much satisfaction.

Before being elected captain he had announced in the *Sangamon Journal*, 15 March, that he was running for the legislature. (He lost the race 6 August.) His election as captain dates from 21 April. The system had the candidates stand still while voters walked to their choices. Intensely disliked, his opponent had no votes at all, leaving the field to Lincoln. Subsequent lore makes his military career seem fun-and-games, but the war was no comic opera. Enlisting for twenty-eight days, his men traversed muck and mire, clothes torn by briers, stumbling upon scenes of recent massacres abuzz with flies and mosquitoes feasting on severed legs and scalped skulls, all festering in the humid heat. Most troops quit at the end of their twenty-eight days, but Lincoln re-enlisted as a private for another twenty days, thereby raising his captain's pay ($110) another $14. In addition, he received warrants for Iowa land—40 acres near Dubuque, to which he added another 120 acres at Council Bluffs in 1860 (Drake 34-35; Lokken 136-38). Son Robert sold what Mary Todd Lincoln called "wild lands in Iowa" in 1892 for $13,000 (Beveridge 1:553n; MTL 265).

APRIL–JULY 1832

He went the campaign, served near three months, met the ordinary hardships of such an expedition, but was in no battle.[3]

It was quite certain I did not break my sword, for I had none to break; but I bent a musket pretty badly on one occasion by accident, but I had a good many bloody struggles with the mosquetoes; and, although I never fainted from loss of blood, I can truly say I was often very hungry.[4]

He and George Harrison were discharged 10 July after Lincoln had mustered out 27 May as captain, 16 June as private in Captain Elijah Iles's company, and now as private in Captain Early's Independent Spy company. On their way home, someone, allegedly "soldiers of our own army," stole their horses. They slogged by foot from Wisconsin until finding a boat at Peoria, but the river was so low they made better time walking, which they did upon reaching Havana—though every step to New Salem meant slipping in the burning sand (W&D 328-29; Whitney 1:544-45). The journey took four days.

Returning from the campaign, and encouraged by his great

popularity among his immediate neighbors, he, the same year, ran for the Legislature.[5]

> In his seven months at New Salem, his only job, other than clerking and postmastering, had been helping to bring in the first steamboat to Springfield on the Sangamon River, indicating his concern for improving the river. Though an anti-Jacksonian in Jackson country, his local concerns easily balanced national politics. Calling himself a Whig meant no more than that he preferred Henry Clay to Andrew Jackson. The obligatory candidate's statement in the *Sagamon Journal* 15 March (an excerpt follows) emphasized the value of opening the river to navigation. Oddly enough, it was "corrected at his request" by John McNamar, commemorated in Lincoln lore as fiancé in absentia of Ann Rutledge (W&D 253).

Considering the great degree of modesty which should always attend youth, it is probable I have already been more presuming than becomes me. However, upon the subjects of which I have treated, I have spoken as I thought. I may be wrong in regards to any or all of them; but holding it a sound maxim, that it is better to be only sometimes right, than at all times wrong, so soon as I discover my opinions to be erroneous, I shall be ready to renounce them.

Every man is said to have his peculiar ambition. Whether it be true or not, I can say for one that I have no other so great as that of being truly esteemed of my fellow men, by rendering myself worthy of their esteem. How far I shall succeed in gratifying this ambition, is yet to be developed. I am young and unknown to many of you. I was born and have ever remained in the most humble walks of life. I have no wealthy or popular relations to recommend me. My case is thrown exclusively upon the independent voters of this county, and if elected they will have conferred a favor upon me, for which I shall be unremitting in my labors to compensate. But if the good people in their wisdom shall see fit to keep me in the back ground, I have been too familiar with disappointments to be very much chagrined.[6]

> Abner Y. Ellis's recollections of Lincoln's first political speech at Island Grove said he would rebut Jacksonians' heckling with his own funny stories. Ellis's rendition of a speech from that first campaign (below) sounds like a misremembered version of the *Sangamon Journal* candidate's statement (above):

"Fellow citizens, I presume you all know who I am. I am humble Abraham Lincoln. I have been solicited by many friends to become a candidate for the legislature. My politics are short and sweet, like the old woman's dance. I am in favor of a national bank. I am in favor of the internal improvement system and a high protective tariff. These are my sentiments and political principles. If elected, I shall be thankful; if not, it will be all the same."[7]

> Ellis, along with the consensus, described Lincoln as a figure of fun on the stump, dressed in calico shirt, flax-and-tow pantaloons six inches too short, coarse tan brogans, blue yarn socks, and old fashioned straw hat (W&D 171; Angle, *Herndon's,* 86). J.R. "Row" Herndon recalled Lincoln's way of replying to heckling about his appearance:

"I have been told that some of my opponents have said that it was a disgrace to the county of Sangamon to have such a looking man as I am stuck up for the Legislature; now, I thought this was a free country, that is the reason I address you today; had I have known to the contrary, I should not have consented to run, but I will say one thing, let the shoe pinch who it may. When I have been a candidate before you some 5 or 6 times and have been beaten every time, I will consider it a disgrace and will be sure never to try it again."[8]

[He] was beaten—his own precinct, however, casting it's votes 277 for and 7 against him. And this too while he was an avowed Clay man, and the precinct the autumn afterwards, giving a majority of 115 to Genl. Jackson over Mr. Clay. This was the only time A was ever beaten on a direct vote of the people.

> Sangamon county returned four representatives to the state legislature. Lincoln was one of eighteen candidates, coming in eighth with 657 votes, 277 of 300 in New Salem precinct. He emphasizes "direct vote," because in 1858 he was beaten by the indirect voting in the state legislature, while still winning a plurality of the direct vote.

August–September 1832

He was now without means and out of business, but was anxious to remain with his friends who had treated him with so much generosity, especially as he had nothing elsewhere to go to. He studied what he should do—thought of learning the black-smith trade—thought of trying to study law—rather thought he could not succeed at that without a better education. Before long, strangely enough, a man offered to sell and did sell, to A. and another as poor as himself, an old stock of goods, upon credit. They opened as merchants; and he says that was *the* store.

He and army friend William Berry went in debt for $750,

taking over a store recently vandalized. They replenished the stock also on credit, and sold dry goods, tools, and liquor—not by drink but in quantity, a distinction important in 1858 debates when Douglas would accuse him of keeping a bar, or "grocery," and Lincoln would insist he "never kept a grocery anywhere in the world" (Thomas, *New Salem*, 60-62; *CW* 3:16).

With at most twenty-five families, New Salem in 1832 had three general stores. Lincoln and Berry took over Reuben Bradford's place. Berry's death in January 1835 left Lincoln responsible for half their debt, but he assumed the whole, calling it "the national debt," which hung over him for ten years (Donald 54; Mearns, *Lincoln Papers*, 1:155).

MAY 1833–JANUARY 1835

Of course they did nothing but get deeper and deeper in debt. He was appointed Postmaster at New-Salem—the office being too insignificant, to make his politics an objection. The store winked out.

William Greene, who owned the building and clerked for Lincoln, helped finance the debt of about a thousand dollars, for, said Greene, Lincoln spent his money to buy a compass for surveying and books, yet paid his half of the notes when they fell due. Greene and other friends covered his other debts (e.g., for a horse, bridle, and saddle to go surveying). The postmastership vanished May 1836 when the post office moved to Petersburg. He should not have been surprised at his appointment in the first place, since Henry Clay chaired the West's postal committee working closely with Jackson's postmaster general, first to hold that office, Kentucky's William T.

Barry (Rich 135-36; Coleman 212). For perspective on Lincoln's debt of $1,000 consider these prices: corn 25 cents a bushel, beef 3 cents a pound; yet during his three years as postmaster he earned only $150 to $175 while surveying earned him only $2.50 a quarter. As legislator he would earn $4.00 a day—"More than I had ever earned in my life" (Pratt, *Personal*, 16). Appointment as a surveyor helped him survive.

6 JANUARY 1834

The Surveyor of Sangamon, offered to depute to A that portion of his work which was within his part of the county. He accepted, procured a compass and chain, studied Flint, and Gibson a little, and went at it. This procured bread, and kept soul and body together.

Neighbor Pollard Simmons recommended Lincoln to the county surveyor, John Calhoun. Both knew he lacked experience, but Calhoun relied on Lincoln's reputation as reliable and a willing learner. He lent him the basic books: Abel Flint, *A System of Geometry and Trigonometry* (Hartford: O. D. Cooke, 1804) and Robert Gibson, *Treatise of Practical Surveying* (9th ed. Philadephia: Joseph Cruckshank, 1808). Gibson offered more theory, with 168 pages of tables suitable for home study—even showing how to improvise instruments and keep proper records. Flint, while acknowledging using Gibson's material, simplified it to be more suitable for field work, including firmly bound fold-outs (Huntington copy 66072 [2d ed., 1808], 32). Along with surveys for Petersburg, Bath, New Boston, and Albany, he surveyed at least three roads, a number of school districts, several farms, and plats for the planned town of Huron. Hearing that a canal was planned to end at Huron, he himself purchased 47 acres (at $1.25 an acre) but sold them the next year when he learned the town would not be built. Worse, his horse was stolen (Baber 2-6, 18). Set by law, his fees amounted to $2.50 per quarter plus $2 for travel. Once he accepted two buck skins to make pants plus a night's lodging (Pratt, *Personal,* 18).

APRIL–AUGUST 1834

The election of 1834 came, and he was then elected to the Legislature by the highest vote cast for any candidate. Major John T. Stuart, then in full practice of the law, was also elected. During the canvass, in a private conversation he encouraged A. study law. After the election he borrowed books of Stuart, took them home with him, and went at it in good earnest. He studied with nobody.[9]

Urged to run by both Bowling Green, the Democratic leader, and John Todd Stuart, the Whig leader, Lincoln announced his candidacy in mid-April and in the August election captured 1,376 votes, hardly "the highest vote," which went to John Dawson (1,390) (Thomas, *New Salem,* 119n). He needed little encouragement to enter politics. Even before leaving Indiana he attended local courts, followed cases in the press, and later borrowed law books from neighbors (Lamon 37; Duff 32). He had served with Stuart in the Black Hawk war. A year older, Stuart had a Kentucky college degree and practiced law in Springfield a few years with Henry E. Dummer but much preferred politics. From Lincoln's later advice to prospective lawyers come hints of the course he himself followed:

Get the books, and read, and study them carefully. Begin with Blackstone's Commentaries, and after reading it carefully through, say twice, take up Chitty's Pleading, Greenleaf's Evidence, and Story's Equity etc. in succession. Work, work, work, is the main thing.[10]

> Except for Blackstone, these were texts of the 30s and 40s. Blackstone's *Commentaries on the Laws of England* had been the basic law book in America since appearing in 1765-70. The four parts treated rights and wrongs, both public and private, premised on the idea that, while laws of nature had precedence, certain legal principles were also fixed and inalienable, reducible to a system. In addition, Blackstone gave the history of English law with precedents and equity. Thomas Chitty's *Forms of Practical Proceedings* (1843) gave models for such documents as wills and deeds. The other texts recommended were by Harvard professors: Simon Greenleaf's *Treatise on the Laws of Evidence* (1842-53) and Joseph Story's *Equity Pleading* (1838). Despite the good advice, the prospective lawyer who received it chose rather to farm in Nebraska (*CW* 4:121n). Isham Reavis, however, did follow the law, profiting from Lincoln's experience:

If you are resolutely determined to make a lawyer of yourself, the thing is more than half done already. It is but a small matter whether you read *with* any body or not.

I did not read with any one. Get the books, and read and study them till, you understand them in their principal features; and that is the main thing. It is of no consequence to be in a large town while you are reading. I read at New-Salem, which never had three hundred people living in it. The *books*, and your *capacity* for understanding them, are just the same in all places.[11]

Stuart described Lincoln's own habits on the circuit during 1844-53:

"In the evening Lincoln would strip off his coat and lay down on the bed—read—reflect and digest—after supper he would strip—go to bed—get a candle—draw up a chair or a table and read till late at night; he read hard books" (Mearns, *Three*, 64). Given the chance to correct Howell's biography, he let stand the description of his reading a copy of Blackstone just bought from an auctioneer "under a wide-spreading tree . . . shifting his position as the sun rose and sank, so as to keep in the shade, and utterly unconscious of everything but the principles of common law. People went by, and he took no account of them" (*Lives* 31).

1836–1837

He still mixed in the surveying to pay board and clothing bills. When the Legislature met, the law books were dropped, but were taken up again at the end of the session. He was re-elected in 1836.[12]

In the 1836 election, Lincoln came in first of a field of seventeen, polling 1,716 votes, while his old patron John Calhoun polled 1,277. Whigs sent seven assemblymen and two senators to the capital, Vandalia, where they were called "the long Nine," in aggregate height totaling 54 feet (Simon 22-27). On the stump Lincoln proved adept at clarifying issues.

13 JUNE 1836

I go for all sharing the privileges of the government, who assist in bearing its burthens. Consequently I go for admitting all whites to the right of suffrage, who pay taxes or bear arms (by no means excluding females). If elected, I shall consider the whole people of Sangamon my constituents, as well those that oppose, as those that support me. While acting as their representative, I shall be governed by their will, on all subjects upon which I have the means of knowing what their will is; and upon all others, I shall do what my own judgment teaches me will best advance their interests.[13]

When one opponent referred to him as a young man, Lincoln counteracted by alluding to his critic as a turn-coat who felt obligated to place a lightning rod on his new house:

"I am not so young in years as I am in the tricks and trades of a politician, but, live long or die young, I would rather die now than, like the gentleman, change my politics and simultaneous with the change, receive an office worth $3,000 a year, and then have to erect a lightning rod over my house to protect a guilty conscience from an offended God."[14]

9 SEPTEMBER 1836

In the autumn of 1836 he obtained a law licence.

Like one-fourth of the legislature, he served before being licensed to practice law. In March he was licensed to practice only in the county; in September, after appearing before two state superior court justices, he could practice in the state. He was not officially enrolled, however, until March 1837. Lack of formal education was no obstacle. West of the Alleghenies there was only one law school. When he was licensed, only four members of the county bar had attended law school or college (Duff 25; Stevens 15-19).

3

SEEKING A FORTUNE
IN SPRINGFIELD

1837–1844

15 APRIL 1837

On April l5, 1837 removed to Springfield, and commenced the practice, his old friend, Stuart taking him into partnership.[1]

> He and Stuart were "boon companions," eating and sleeping together in the same boarding house. Both active supporters of Henry Clay, they served on the same assembly committees. They later split on the slavery issue. But meanwhile, Stuart left the routine practice to Lincoln while he played Whig leader. In the legislature, Lincoln said little the first year but, a good committeeman, made many friends, a valuable asset in moving the capital to Springfield, his home until leaving for Washington. Approaching thirty years of age, he thought about taking a wife, as narrated in his letters to a neighbor's sister, Mary Owens of Kentucky. Like ill-fated and unmentioned Ann Rutledge, she was of medium height but more rotund and, like Mary Todd, had a first-class education.

Mary Todd, his law partner's cousin, was also sister-in-law of Ninian W. Edwards, power broker in Illinois Whig politics. In subsequently wedding Mary Todd, Lincoln gave political opponents a clear shot at accusing him of being a member of the Establishment. They were not far from wrong, for Mary Todd Lincoln, as mother of his sons, helpmate, and mentor, helped him develop as leader of his party and leading railroad lawyer in the Middle West. Meanwhile he was handling twenty-five to thirty cases each term, and in April 1841 would join the more scholarly Judge Stephen T. Logan (Angle, *100 Years* 17, 11-22; Duff, 74-79).

7 MAY 1837

Springfield, May 7, 1837
Friend Mary [Owens]

I have commenced two letters to send you before this, both of which displeased me before I got half done, and so I tore them up. The first I thought wasn't serious enough, and the second was on the other extreme. I shall send this, turn out as it may.

This thing of living in Springfield is rather a dull business after all, at least it is so to me. I am quite as lonesome here as ever was anywhere in my life. I have been spoken to by but one woman since I've been here, and should not have been by her, if she could have avoided it. I've never been to church yet, nor probably shall not be soon. I stay away because I am conscious I should not know how to behave myself.

I am often thinking about what we said of your coming to live in Springfield. I am afraid you would not be satisfied. There is a great deal of flourishing about in carriages here, which it would be your doom to see without shareing in it. You would have to be poor without the means of hiding your poverty. Do you believe you could bear that patiently? Whatever woman may cast her lot with mine, should any ever do so, it is my intention to do all in my power to make her happy and contented; and there is nothing I can immagine, that would make me more unhappy than to fail in the effort. I know I should be much happier with you than the way I am, provided I saw no signs of discontent in you. What you have said to me may have been in jest, or I may have misunderstood it. If so, then let it be forgotten; if otherwise, I much wish you would think seriously before you decide. For my part I have already decided. What I have said I will most positively abide by, provided you wish it. My opinion is that you had better not do it. You have not been accustomed to hardship, and it may be more severe than you now immagine. I know you are capable of thinking correctly on any subject; and if you deliberate maturely upon this, before you decide, then I am willing to abide your decision.

You must write me a good long letter after you get this. You have nothing else to do, and though it might not seem interesting to you, after you had written it, it would be a good deal of company to me in this "busy wilderness."

Yours, etc. LINCOLN[2]

August 1837

Springfield Aug. 16 1837
Friend Mary.
    You will, no doubt, think it rather strange, that I should

write you a letter on the same day on which we parted; and I can only account for it by supposing, that seeing you lately makes me think of you more than usual, while at our late meeting we had but few expressions of thoughts. You must know that I can not see you, or think of you, with entire indifference; and yet it may be, that you, are mistaken in regard to what my real feelings towards you are. If I knew you were not, I should not trouble you with this letter. Perhaps any other man would know enough without further information; but I consider it *my* peculiar right to plead ignorance, and your bounden duty to allow the plea. I want in all cases to do right, and most particularly so, in all cases with women. I want, at this particular time, more than any thing else, to do right with you, and if I *knew* it would be doing right, as I rather suspect it would, to let you alone, I would do it. And for the purpose of making the matter as plain as possible, I now say, that you can now drop the subject, dismiss your thoughts (if you ever had any) from me forever, and leave this letter unanswered, without calling forth one accusing murmer from me. And I will even go further, and say, that if it will add any thing to your comfort, or peace of mind, to do so, it is my sincere wish that you should. Do not understand by this, that I wish to cut your acquaintance. I mean no such thing. What I do wish is, that our further acquaintance shall depend upon yourself. If such further acquaintance would contribute nothing to your happiness, I am sure it would not to mine. If you feel yourself in any degree bound to me, I am now willing to release you, provided you wish it; while, on the other hand, I am willing, and even anxious to bind you faster, if I can be convinced that it will, in any considerable degree, add to your happiness. This, indeed, is the whole question with me. Nothing would make me more miserable than to believe you miserable—nothing more happy, than to know you were so.

In what I have now said, I think I can not be misunderstood; and to make myself understood, is the only object of this letter.

If it suits you best to not answer this—farewell—a long life and a merry one attend you. But if you conclude to write back, speak as plainly as I do. There can be neither harm nor danger, in saying, to me, any thing you think, just in the manner you think it. Your friend LINCOLN[3]

> He summarized the romantic interlude (below) for Eliza Caldwell Browning, a Vandalia friend who apparently helped him with letter writing. Mary Owens would later say that, though generally true, the story ended because of a personality conflict. When told he had said she "was a great fool" for not marrying him, she replied, "Characteristic of the man." (W&D 263)

1 APRIL 1838

Without appologising for being egotistical, I shall make the history of so much of my own life, as has elapsed since I saw you, the subject of this letter. And by the way I now discover, that, in order to give a full and inteligible account of the things I have done and suffered *since* I saw you, I shall necessarily have to relate some that happened *before*.

It was, then, in the autumn of 1836, that a married lady of my acquaintance, and who was a great friend of mine, being about to pay a visit to her father and other relatives residing in Kentucky, proposed to me, that on her return she would bring a sister of hers with her, upon condition that I would engage to become her brother-in-law with all convenient dispach. I, of course, accepted the proposal; for you know I could not have done otherwise, had I really been averse to it; but privately between you and me, I was most confoundedly well pleased with the project. I had seen the said sister some three years before, thought her inteligent and agreeable, and saw no good objection to plodding life through hand in hand with her. Time passed on, the lady took her journey and in due time returned, sister in company sure enough. This stomached me a little; for it appeared to me, that her coming so readily showed that she was a trifle too willing; but on reflection it occured to me, that she might have been prevailed on by her married sister to come, without any thing concerning me ever having been mentioned to her; and so I concluded that if no other objection presented itself, I would consent to wave this. All this occured upon my *hearing* of her arrival in the neighbourhood; for, be it remembered, I had not yet *seen* her, except about three years previous, as before mentioned.

In a few days we had an interview, and although I had seen her before, she did not look as my immagination had pictured her. I knew she was over-size, but she now appeared a fair match for Falstaff; I knew she was called an "old maid," and I felt no doubt of the truth of at least half of the appelation; but now, when I beheld her, I could not for my life avoid thinking of my mother; and this, not from withered features, for her skin was too full of fat, to permit its contracting in to wrinkles; but from her want of teeth, weather-beaten appearance in general, and from a kind of notion that ran in my head, that *nothing* could have commenced at the size of infancy, and reached her present bulk in less than thirtyfive or forty years; and, in short, I was not all pleased with her. But what could I do? I had told her sister that I would take her for better or for worse;

and I made a point of honor and conscience in all things, to stick to my word, especially if others had been induced to act on it, which in this case, I doubted not they had, for I was now fairly convinced, that no other man on earth would have her, and hence the conclusion that they were bent on holding me to my bargain. Well, thought I, I have said it, and, be consequences what they may, it shall not be my fault if I fail to do it. At once I determined to consider her my wife; and this done, all my powers of discovery were put to the rack, in search of perfections in her, which might be fairly set-off against her defects. I tried to immagine she was handsome, which, but for her unfortunate corpulency, was actually true. Exclusive of this, no woman that I have seen, has a finer face. I also tried to convince myself, that the mind was much more to be valued than the person; and in this, she was not inferior, as I could discover, to any with whom I had been acquainted.

Shortly after this, without attempting to come to any positive understanding with her, I set out for Vandalia, where and when you first saw me. During my stay there, I had letters from her, which did not change my opinion of either her intelect or intention; but on the contrary, confirmed it in both.

All this while, although I was fixed "firm as the surge repelling rock" in my resolution, I found I was continually repenting the rashness, which had led me to make it. Through life I have been in no bondage, either real or immaginary from the thraldom of which I so much desired to be free.

After my return home, I saw nothing to change my opinion of her in any particular. She was the same and so was I. I now spent my time between planing how I might get along through life after my contemplated change of circumstances should have taken place; and how I might procrastinate the evil day for a time, which I really dreaded as much—perhaps more, than an irishman does the halter.

After all my suffering upon this deeply interesting subject . . . I got out of it. Out clear in every sense of the term; no violation of word, honor or conscience . . . As the lawyers say, it was done in the manner following, to wit—

After I had delayed the matter as long as I thought I could in honor do, which by the way had brought me round into the last fall, I concluded I might as well bring it to a consumation without further delay; and so I mustered my resolution, and made the proposal to her direct; but, shocking to relate, she answered, No.

At first I supposed she did it through an affectation of modesty, which I thought but ill-become her, under the peculiar circumstances of her case; but on my renewal of the charge, I found she repeled it with greater firmness than before. I tried it again and again, but with the same success, or rather with the same want of success. I finally was forced to give it up, at which I verry unexpectedly found myself mortified almost beyond endurance.

I was mortified, it seemed to me, in a hundred different ways. My vanity was deeply wounded by the reflection, that I had so long been too stupid to discover her intentions, and at the same time never doubting that I understood them perfectly; and also, that she whom I had taught myself to believe no body else would have, had actually rejected me with all my fancied greatness, and to cap the whole, I then, for the first time, began to suspect that I was really a little in love with her.

But let it all go. I'll try and out live it. Others have been made fools of by the girls; but this can never be with truth said of me. I most emphatically, in this instance, made a fool of myself. I have now come to the conclusion never again to think of marrying; and for this reason; I can never be satisfied with anyone who would be block-head enough to have me.[4]

A year older than Lincoln, with fair skin, deep blue eyes, dark curling hair and at 5'5" weighing 150 pounds, Mary Owens considered Lincoln beneath her, at least in intellect. Daughter of the headmaster of Kentucky's "Rural Academy," she believed few persons her equal in that regard. Later, she confessed to have angered him when he visited, by telling a boy to fib that she was not home when Lincoln knew she was home. Still, she said there were no "hard feelings towards each other that I knew of" (Pond 20; W&D 262, 530, 610).

The third letter above, the one to Elizabeth Caldwell Browning, seems meant to be an exercise in composition for her correction. A similar exercise, reporting a bizarre case of "murder" in a letter to Joshua Speed, 19 June 1841 (below) would be expanded five years later for the Quincy *Whig* (*CW* 1: 371-76). Mrs. Browning, newly wed to Lincoln's friend and fellow boarder Orville Browning, hosted Lincoln in their rooms at Vandalia on many an evening. She thought the letter "written in a droll and amusing vein" and laughed at it for years to come, until the President assured her "that there was much more truth in that letter than she supposed" (Nicolay 4). Dating the letter "April 1," All Fools Day, however, justifies her amusement. The expression "firm as the surge repelling rock," is said to have appeared on the frontispiece of David Ramsay's popular *Life of Washington* (2nd ed., Boston: D. Mallory, 1811), but is in neither of the Huntington Library's copies, accession numbers 78867 or 94285 (Warren 162).

3 March 1837

By a protest entered upon the Ills. House Journal of that date, at pages 817, 818, A. with Dan Stone, another representative of Sangamon, briefly defined his position on the slavery question; and so far as it goes, it was then the same that it is now:[5]

"They believe that the institution of slavery is founded on both injustice and bad policy; but that the promulgation of abolition doctrines tends rather to increase than to abate its evils.

"They believe that the Congress of the United States has no power, under the constitution, to interfere with the institution of slavery in the different States.

"They believe that the Congress of the United States has the power, under the constitution, to abolish slavery in the District of Columbia; but that that power ought not to be exercised unless at the request of the people of said District."[6]

> Native Vermonter, one of the Long Nine, Dan Stone joined Lincoln's protest. Four others protested, but only Lincoln and Stone objected formally in the House Journal, not a politic move at the time, for sentiment against abolitionists peaked with the murder of Elijah Lovejoy (Simon, 132-33; Pease 363-69; Power 690). The petition would have been timely in January, but they delayed it to avoid diversion from lobbying efforts to move the capital to Springfield.

1838, 1840

He was re-elected in 1836, 1838, and 1840. . . . In 1838 and 1840 Mr. L's party in the Legislature voted for him as

Speaker; but being in the minority, he was not elected. After 1840, he declined a re-election to the Legislature.[7]

> Lincoln misremembered the makeup of the legislature. Whigs had a majority in the Senate and in the House, yet his Democratic opponent for the speakership outpolled Lincoln 43 to 38 in 1838 and defeated him again in 1840 when Whigs had a majority of 46 to 45. By that time, his lack of interest appears in his absences—92 in the last session of 1840 versus colleagues' average of 53.7, while two returns in 1840 showed him trailing his party at the polls (Simon 150, 206, 271).

1840

I do not think my prospects individually are very flattering, for I think it is probable I shall not be permitted to be a candidate.[8]

> To counter voters' rejection of "the Springfield junto's" power in the legislature, Lincoln stumped the countryside with Edward D. Baker, a better debater but one who depended on Lincoln's ghost-writing even for legislation. The Lincolns named their second son after him (Beveridge 1:270-74).

1841

"The gentleman had accused old women of being partial to the number 9; but this he presumed was without foundation. A few years since, it would be recollected by the House, that the delegation from this county were dubbed, by way of eminence, 'the long nine,' and by way of further distinction, he had been called the 'longest' of the nine. 'Now' said Mr. L. 'I desire to say . . . that if any woman, old or young, ever thought there was any peculiar charm in this distinguished specimen of number 9, I have, as yet, been so unfortunate as not to have discovered it.'"[9]

Headed, "Lincoln's Speech in 1841," this transcript in the Huntington Library's Herndon papers (LN2408, 3: 555-56) purports to record a jocular speech related to debates on reapportionment (*Journal of 12th General Assembly* [Springfield: Walters, 1841] 219, 295, 350). Lincoln opposed creating new counties thus adding to legislators. When he entered in 1834 there were 55; by 1841 they numbered 91 (Simon 243).

20 JANUARY 1841

I have within the last few days, been making a most discreditable exhibition of myself in the way of hypochondriaism and thereby got an impression that Dr. Henry is necessary to my existence.[10]

Dr. Anson G. Henry offered moral and physician's support following the traumatic breaking of Lincoln's engagement to Mary Todd. When he found himself lusting for her brother-in-law's cousin, Lincoln confessed the illicit passion to Mary, who saw the wisdom of the break (D. Wilson, *Honor's,* 225-27). Friends described his subsequent depression as "two Cat fits and a Duck fit," serious enough for Joshua Speed to remove him to the Speeds' ancestral Kentucky home for supervised care (D. Wilson, "Fatal," 101-30).

23 JANUARY 1841

I am now the most miserable man living. If what I feel were equally distributed to the whole human family, there would not be one cheerful face on the earth. Whether I shall ever be better I can not tell; I awfully forbode I shall not. To remain as I am is impossible; I must die or be better. I fear I shall be unable to attend to any bussiness here, and a change of scene might help me.[11]

> But a change of scene was not to be. His friend Speed had moved to the ancestral home near Louisville, but the change of scene had to be delayed as Lincoln, assuring him he was "neither dead, nor quite crazy yet" (Miers 1:153), immersed "his cares among the intricacies and perplexities of the law" (Sandburg 180), including the bizarre case of presumed murder which he reported in mid-June and five years later for the press.

19 JUNE 1841

The chief personages in the drama, are Archibald Fisher, supposed to be murdered; and Archibald Trailor, Henry Trailor, and William Trailor, supposed to have murdered him. The three Trailors were brothers; The first, Arch, lives in town; the second, Henry, in Clary's Grove, and the third Wm, in Warren County; and Fisher, the supposed *murderee*, being without a family, had made his home with William.

On saturday evening, being the 29th of May, Fisher and William came to Henry's in a one-horse dearborn [buggy] and there staid over sunday; and on monday, all three came to Springfield, Henry on horseback, and joined Archibald at Myers' the Dutch carpenter. That evening at supper Fisher was missing, and so next morning. Some ineffectual search was made for him; and on tuesday at 1 p.m. Wm and Henry started home without him.

In a day or so Henry and one or two of his Clary Grove

neighbours came back and searched for him again, and advertised his disappearance in the paper. The knowledge of the matter thus far, had not been general; and here it dropped entirely till about the 10th inst. when [Postmaster] Keys received a letter from the Post Master in Warren [County], stating that Wm had arrived at home, and was telling a verry mysterious and improbable story about the disappearance of Fisher, which induced the community there to suppose that he had been disposed of unfairly.

Keys made this letter public, which immediately set the whole town and adjoining country agog . . . The mass of the People commenced a systematic search for the dead body, while [Deputy] Wickersham was dispatched to arrest Henry Trailor at the Grove; and [Deputy] Maxey, to Warren to arrest William. On Monday Henry was brought in and showed an evident inclination to insinuate that he knew Fisher to be dead, and that Arch and Wm had killed him. He said he guessed the body could be found in Spring Creek between the Beardstown road bridge and Hickoxes mill.

Away the People swept like a herd of buffaloes, and cut down Hickoxes mill dam *nolens volens,* to draw water out of the pond; and then went up and down, and down and up the creek, fishing and raking, and ducking and diving for two days, and after all, no dead body found.

In the mean time a sort of scuffling ground had been found in the brush in the angle or point where the road leading into the woods past the brewery, and the one leading in past the brickyard join. From this scuffle ground, was the sign of something about the size of a man having been dragged to the edge of the thicket, where it joined the track of some small wheeled carriage which was drawn by one horse, as shown by the horse tracks. The carriage track led off towards Spring Creek.

Near this drag trail, Dr. Merryman found *two hairs,* which after a long scientific examination, he pronounced to be triangular human hairs, which term, he says includes within it the whiskers, the hairs growing under the arms and on other parts of the body; and he judged that these two were of the whiskers, because the ends were cut, showing that they had flourished in the neighbourhood of the razor's opperations . . .

William was put upon his examining trial—Logan, Baker, and your humble servant defended. Henry was then introduced by the prossecution. He swore, that when they had started for home, they went out North and turned down West by the brick yard into the woods, and there met Archibald; that they proceeded a small distance further, where he was placed as a sentinel to watch for, and announce the approach of any one that might happen that way; that William and Arch took the dearborn out of the road a small distance to the edge of the thicket, where they stopped, and he saw them lift the body of a man into it; that they then moved off with the carriage in the direction of Hicoxes mill, and he loitered about for something like an hour, when William returned with the carriage, but without Arch and said that they had put *him* in a safe place; that they then went some how, he did not know exactly how, into the road close to the brewery, and proceeded on to Clary's Grove. He also stated that sometime during the day, William told him, that he and Arch had killed Fisher the evening before; that the way they did it was by him (William) knocking him down with a club, and Arch then choking him to death.

An old man from Warren, called Dr. Gilmore, was then introduced on the part of the defence. He swore that he had known Fisher for several years; that Fisher had resided at his house a long time at each of two different spells; once while he built a barn for him, and once while he was doctored for some chronic disease; that two or three years ago, Fisher had a serious hurt in his head by the bursting of a gun, since which he has been subject to continual bad health, and occasional abberations of mind.

He also stated that on last Tuesday, being the same day that Maxey arrested William Trailor, he (the Doctor) was from home in the early part of the day, and on his return about 11 o'clock, found Fisher at his house in bed, and apparantly verry unwell; that he asked how he had come from Springfield; that Fisher said he had come by Peoria, and also told several other places he had been at not in the direction of Peoria, which showed that he, at the time of speaking, did not know where he had been, or that he had been wandering about in a state of derangement.

He further stated that in about two hours he received a note from one of William Trailor's friends, advising him of his arrest, and requesting him to go to Springfield as a witness, to testify to the state of Fisher's health in former times; that he immediately set off catching up two of his neighbours, as company, and riding all evening and all night, overtook Maxey and William at Lewiston in Fulton County; that Maxey refusing to discharge Trailor upon his statement, his two neighbors returned, and he came on to Springfield.

Some question being made whether the doctor's story was not a fabrication, several acquaintances of his, among whom was the same Post Master who wrote to Keys as before mentioned, were introduced as sort of compurgators, who all swore, that they knew the Doctor be of good character for truth and veracity, and generally of good character in every way. Here the testimony ended, and the Trailors were discharged, Arch and William expressing, both in word and manner their entire confidence that Fisher would be found alive at the doctor's ... while Henry still protested that no power on earth could ever show Fisher alive.

Thus stands this curious affair now. When the doctor's story was first made public, it was amusing to scan and contemplate the countenances, and hear the remarks of those who had been actively engaged in the search for the dead body. Some looked quizical, some melancholly, and some furiously angry. Porter, who had been very active, swore he always knew the man was not dead, and that *he* had not stirred an inch to hunt for him; Langford, who had taken the lead in cuting down Hicox's mill dam, and wanted to hang Hickox for objecting, looked most awfully wo-begone; he seemed the "*wictim of hunrequited haffection*" as represented in the comic almanic we used to laugh over; and Hart, the little drayman that hauled Molly home once, said it was too *damned* bad, to have so much trouble, and no hanging after all.[12]

> For three weeks in August he visited Speed's ancestral home. His friend Joshua Speed was a direct descendant of Joshua Fry, partner in mapmaking with Thomas Jefferson's father and also George Washington's commanding officer in the French-Indian war; another ancestor was Thomas Walker who had been Jefferson's guardian and Washington's partner in land jobbing. Back in Springfield, Lincoln wrote a thank-you letter describing the voyage home, a voyage evoking powerful emotions thereafter.

September 1841

We got on board the Steam Boat Lebanon, in the locks of the Canal about 12 o'clock noon of the day we left, and reached St. Louis the next Monday at 8 p.m. Nothing of interest happened during the passage, except the vexatious delays occasioned by the sand bars be thought interesting. By the way, a fine example was presented on board the boat for contemplating the effect of *condition* upon human happiness. A gentleman had purchased twelve negroes in diferent parts of Kentucky and was taking them to a farm in the South. They were chained six and six together. A small iron clevis was around the left wrist of each, and this fastened to the main chain by a shorter one at a convenient distance from the others; so that the negroes were strung together precisely like so many fish upon a trot-line. In this condition they were being separated forever from the scenes of their childhood, their friends, their fathers and mothers, and brothers and sisters, and many of them, from their wives and children, and going into perpetual slavery where the lash of the master is proverbially more ruthless and unrelenting than any other where; and yet amid all these distressing circumstances, as we would think them, they were the most cheerful and apparantly happy creatures on board. One, whose offence for which he had been sold was an over-fondness for his wife, played the fiddle almost continually; and the others danced, sung, cracked jokes, and played various games with cards from day to day. How true it is that "God tempers the wind to the shorn lamb," or in other words, that He renders the worst of human conditions tolerable, while He permits the best, to be nothing better than tolerable.[13]

From Louisville to the mouth of the Ohio, there were, on board, ten or a dozen slaves, shackled together with irons. That sight was a continual torment to me; and I see someting like it every time I touch the Ohio, or any other slave border.[14]

For much of 1842 an exchange of letters with Speed meditated on love and marriage, particularly such indecision in marrying he himself had felt as he now commiserated with Speed, as if talking to himself:

3 JANUARY 1842

You say you *reasoned* yourself into it. What do you mean by that? Was it not, that you found yourself unable to *reason* yourself *out* of it? Did you not think, and partly form the purpose, of courting her the first time you ever saw or heard of her? What had reason to do with it, at that early stage? There was nothing *at that time* for reason to work upon. Whether she was moral, aimiable, sensible, or even of good character, you did not, nor could not then know; except perhaps you might infer the last from the company you found her in. All you then did or could know of her, was her *personal appearance* and *deportment;* and these, if they impress at all, impress the *heart* and not the head.[15]

25 FEBRUARY 1842

It is the peculiar misfortune of both you and me, to dream dreams of Elysium far exceeding all that any thing earthly can realize. Far short of your dreams as you may be, no woman could do more to realize them, than that same black eyed Fanny. If you could but contemplate her through my immagination, it would appear ridiculous to you, that any one should for a moment think of being unhappy with her. My old Father used to have a saying that "If you make a bad bargain, *hug* it the tighter"; and it occurs to me, that if the bargain you have just closed can possibly be called a bad one, it is certainly the most *pleasant one* for applying the maxim to, which my fancy can, by any effort, picture.[16]

4 JULY 1842

Before I resolve to do the one thing or the other, I must regain my confidence in my own ability to keep my resolves when they are made. In that ability, you know, I once prided myself as the only, or at least the chief, gem of my character; that gem I lost—how, and when, you too well know. I have not yet regained it; and until I do, I can not trust myself in any matter of much importance. I always was superstitious; and as part of my superstition, I believe God made me one of the instruments of bringing your Fanny and you together, which union, I have no doubt He had fore-ordained. Whatever he designs, he will do for *me* yet. "Stand *still* and see the salvation of the Lord" is my text just now.[17]

5 OCTOBER 1842

"Are you now, in *feeling* as well as *judgement,* glad you are married as you are?"

From any body but me, this would be an impudent question not to be tolerated; but I know you will pardon it in me. Please answer it quickly as I feel impatient to know.[18]

> Having talked Speed through the conflict between head and heart resolving in marriage, Lincoln again faced grievous indecision as he and Mary Todd became close once more. On one occasion he took the blame for her lampoons of fiery James Shields, whose challenge to a duel was averted by Lincoln's assuring him that the satire

was not personal but political. But he did go so far as to draw up preliminary groundrules. Late in life, asked to talk about the duel, he said: "If you desire my friendship, you will never mention it again" (MTL 299).

19 September 1842

The preliminaries of the fight are to be—1st Weapons—Cavalry broad swords of the largest size, precisely equal in all respects—and such as now used by the cavalry company at Jacksonville. 2nd. Position—A plank ten feet long, and from nine to twelve inches broad to be firmly fixed on edge, on the ground, as the line between us which neither is to pass his foot over upon forfeit of his life . . .[19]

4 November 1842

Nothing new here, except my marrying, which to me, is matter of profound wonder.[20]

> The entire affair was secret, courting at Dr. Anson Henry's and marrying in the Ninian Edwards's parlor—despite the antipathy of Elizabeth Todd Edwards, who felt Mary could have done better. The bride wore a white satin gown borrowed from sister Frances, with bridesmaids Mary Lamb and Julia Jayne. As the groom left his boarding house, a little boy asked, "Where are you going?" and he is supposed to have sighed, "To Hell, sonny!" (Roberts 28; Hunt 237). The best man was James H. Matheny, fellow attorney and fervent follower of Henry Clay.

In November 1842 he was married to Mary, daughter of Robert S. Todd, of Lexington, Kentucky. They have three living children—one born in 1843, one in 1850, and one in 1853. They lost one, who was born in 1846.[21]

Lincoln's entries in the family Bible show birth dates for all three sons and death date for baby Eddie ("February 1, 1850") along with the date of his marriage to Mary Todd. Robert would later extend entries with death dates for Willie ("20 February 1862") and Tad ("15 July 1871"). This Bible, *Comprehensive Bible* (Philadelphia: Lippincott, 1847), is often confused with another "family Bible" belonging to his stepmother (London: SPCK, 1799) reproduced in Barrett, *Immortal,* item 99. Lincoln's Bible was exhibited in the Library of Congress (catalogue entry 33, 1959) (*CW* 1:304).

14 FEBRUARY 1843

If you should hear any one say that Lincoln didn't want to go to Congress, I wish you as a personal friend of mine, would tell him you have reason to believe he is mistaken. The truth is, I would like to go very much. Still, circumstances may happen which may prevent my being a candidate. If there are any who be my friends in such an enterprise, what I now want is that they shall not throw me away just yet.[22]

With reapportionment based on the 1840 census, new congressional seats were added to his district, so Lincoln tested the waters with such letters as this one to Richard Thomas Jr., who had strong Whig connections in the Midwest and later became an influential editor of the radical Republican press who vigorously supported Lincoln for president (Snyder 524-25). At this time, however, Whigs were hopelessly split on such issues as internal improvements favored by those in the northern part of the state and slavery insisted upon by those in the southern part. Concerned party leaders therefore met in Springfield to hammer out a policy acceptable to both sides, delegating the drafting to Lincoln's partner Stephen T. Logan, his close neighbor Albert Taylor Bledsoe, and Lincoln himself (Thompson 120).

The allusions to Aesop and *Mark* 3:25 are apt because both refer to dissension—Aesop telling of the father who teaches the family by having them try in vain to break a whole bundle of sticks rather than one at a time; *Mark* drawing the parallel between divided house and divided kingdom:

4 MARCH 1843

That "union is strength" is a truth that has been known, illustrated and declared, in various ways and forms in all ages of the world. That great fabulist and philosopher, Aesop, illustrated it by his fable of the bundle of sticks; and he whose wisdom surpasses that of all philosophers, has declared that "a house divided against itself cannot stand." If two friends aspire to the same office, it is certain both cannot succeed. Would it not, then, be much less painful to have the question decided by mutual friends some time before, than to snarl and quarrel till the day of election, and then both be beaten by the common enemy?[23]

> Successful in persuading Whigs to nominate by convention, Lincoln nevertheless lost in his home district's convention. He was nominated by the Menard County convention. Sangamon County delegates backed Edward D. Baker, and Lincoln broke a tie between Baker and John J. Hardin by suggesting that all three of them take turns as Whig nominees for the new Seventh District seat (Riddle, *Lincoln Runs*, 71-72).

24 MARCH 1843

We had a meeting of the Whigs of the county here on last monday to appoint delegates to a district convention, and Baker beat me and got the delegation instructed to go for him. The meeting, in spite of my attempt to decline it, appointed me one of the delegates; so that in getting Baker the nomination, I shall be "fixed" a good deal like a fellow who is made groomsman to the man what has cut him out, and is marrying his own dear "gal."[24]

26 MARCH 1843

It is truly gratifying to me to learn that while the people of Sangamon have cast me off, my old friends of Menard who have known me longest and best of any, still retain there confidence in me. It would astonish if not amuse, the older citizens of your County who twelve years ago knew me a strange, friendless, uneducated, penniless boy, working on a flat boat at ten dollars per month to learn that I have been put down here as the candidate of pride, wealth, and aristocratic family distinction. Yet so chiefly it was. My wife has some relatives in the Presbyterian and some in the Episcopal Churches, and therefore, wherever it would tell, I was set down as either the one or the other, whilst it was every where contended that no christian ought to go for me, because I belonged to no church, was suspected of being a deist, and had talked about fighting a duel.[25]

18 MAY 1843

We are not keeping house; but boarding at the Globe tavern, which is very well kept now by a widow lady of the name of Beck. Our room and boarding only costs four dollars a week. I reckon it will scarcely be in our power to visit Kentucky this year. Besides poverty, and the necessity of attending to business, those "coming events" I suspect would be some what in the way.[26]

> Chief "coming event" was birth of Robert Todd Lincoln. Since the parents had no nurse, Sophie Bledsoe, age six, served as babysitter, while her mother, "who never cared personally for Mrs. Lincoln," looked after them. The Bledsoes lived in the same boarding house that Sophie called a "primitive sort—a big, ugly frame building" with a bell that rang for arriving stage coaches and doubtlessly woke the baby. But considering Lincoln's income of $100 a week, the rent of $4.00, even if that meant $4.00 apiece, made possible saving for a house and paying off debts (Sophie B. Herrick, "Personal Recollections," q. R.R. Wilson 61; Angle, *Here*, 87; Pratt, *Personal*, 83-84).

1 AUGUST 1843

"When my wife had her first baby, the doctor from time to time reported to me that everything was going on as well as could be expected under the circumstances. That satisfied me *he* was doing his best, but still I felt anxious to hear the first squall. It came at last, and I felt mightily relieved."[27]

> Neither infant nor law practice could stay Lincoln from political rounds. As an elector he with a Democratic elector followed the court around its circuit. David Davis described the routine: "The afternoon is occupied by the two Presidential Electors in political discussion each speaking about 3 hours. Sometimes they keep up the talk, every night during the week," with Lincoln being "the best Stump Speaker in the State." Replied Davis's father-

in-law, "No wonder your public men are good speakers. They are eternally talking" (King 47).

OCTOBER 1844

In the fall of 1844, thinking I might aid some to carry the State of Indiana for Mr. Clay, I went into the neighborhood in that State in which I was raised, where my mother and only sister were buried, and from which I had been absent about fifteen years. That part of the country is, within itself, as unpoetical as any spot of the earth; but still, seeing it and its objects and inhabitants aroused feelings in me which were certainly poetry; though whether my expression of those feelings is poetry is quite another question. To say the least, I am not at all displeased to publish the poetry, or doggerel, or whatever else it may be called. I have not sufficient hope of the verses attracting any favorable notice to tempt me to risk being ridiculed for having written them. The subject is an insane man. His name is Matthew Gentry. He is three years older than I, and when we were boys we went to school together. He was rather a bright lad, and *the* son of the rich man of our very poor neighbourhood. At the age of nineteen he unaccountably became furiously mad, from which condition he gradually settled down into harmless insanity. I found him still lingering in this wretched condition. In my poetizing mood I could not forget the impressions his case made upon me. Here is the result-

My childhood-home I see again,
    And gladden with the view;
And still as mem'ries crowd my brain,
    There's sadness in it too—

O memory! thou mid-way world
   'Twixt Earth and Paradise,
Where things decayed, and loved ones lost
   In dreamy shadows rise—

And freed from all that's gross or vile,
   Seem hallowed, pure, and bright,
Like scenes in some enchanted isle,
   All bathed in liquid light—

As distant mountains please the eye,
   When twilight chases day—
As bugle-tones, that, passing by,
   In distance die away.

As leaving some grand water-fall
   We ling'ring list it's roar,
So memory will hallow all
   We've known, but know no more—

Now twenty years have passed away,
   Since here I bid farewell
To woods, and fields, and scenes of play
   And school-mates loved so well—

Where many were, how few remain
   Of old familiar things!
But seeing these to mind again
   The lost and absent brings—

The friends I left that parting day—
   How changed, as time has sped!
Young childhood grown, strong manhood grey,
   And half of all are dead—

I hear the lone survivors tell
    How nought from death could save,
Till every sound appears a knell,
    And every spot a grave.—

I range the fields with pensive tread,
    I pace the hollow rooms;
And feel (companion of the dead)
    I'm living in the tombs—

And here's an object more of dread
    Than ought the grave contains—
A human-form, with reason fled,
    While wretched life remains.—

Poor Matthew! Once of genius bright,—
    A fortune-favored child—
Now locked for aye, in mental night,
    A haggard mad-man wild—

Poor Matthew! I have ne'er forgot
    When first with maddened will,
Yourself you maimed, your father fought,
    And mother strove to kill;

And terror spread, and neighbours ran,
    Your dang'rous strength to bind;
And soon a howling crazy man,
    Your limbs were fast confined—

How then you writhed and shrieked aloud,
    Your bones and sinnews bared;
And fiendish on the gaping crowd,
    With burning eye-balls glared—

And begged, and swore, and wept, and prayed,
   With maniac laughter joined—
How fearful are the signs displayed,
   By pangs that kill the mind!

And when at length, tho' drear and long,
   Time soothed your fiercer woes—
How plaintively your mournful song,
   Upon the still night rose-

I've heard it oft, as if I dreamed,
   Far-distant, sweet, and lone;
The funeral dirge it ever seemed
   Of reason dead and gone-

To drink it's strains, I've stole away,
   All silently and still,
Ere yet the rising god of day
   Had streaked the Eastern hill-

But this is past, and nought remains
   That raised you o'er the brute.
Your mad'ning shrieks and soothing strains
   Are like forever mute-

Now fare thee well. More thou the cause
   Than subject now of woe.
All mental pangs, by time's kind laws,
   Hast lost the power to know-

And now away to seek some scene
   Less painful than the last—
With less of horror mingled in
   The present and the past-

The very spot where grew the bread
  That formed my bones, I see.
How strange, old field, on thee to tread,
  And feel I'm part of thee![28]

Usually Lincoln would secrete such verse in his office
drawer (D. Wilson, *Lincoln Before,* 141). Yet he was
willing enough to publish these lines plus another set
describing a bear hunt, verse apparently recited during a
speech, for the *Indiana Daily Sentinel* of 20 September
1852 recalled it as "a graphic account of a bear hunt in
the early days of this wonder country, when the barking
of dogs, the yelling of men, and the cracking of the rifle
when Bruin was treed, would send the blood bounding
through the veins of the pioneer" (Wiley 14). In a
remarkable foretelling of William Faulkner's short story
masterpiece, "The Bear," Lincoln is reported as concluding: "He did not think any other state of society would
ever exist where men would be drawn so close together
in feeling and affection."

A wild-bear chace, didst never see?
  Then hast thou lived in vain.
Thy richest bump of glorious glee,
  Lies desert in thy brain.

When first my father settled here,
  'Twas then the frontier line:
The panther's scream, filled night with fear
  And bears preyed on the swine.

But wo for Bruin's short lived fun,
  When rose the squealing cry;
Now man and horse, with dog and gun,
  For vengeance, at him fly.

A sound of danger strikes his ear;
   He gives the breeze a snuff:
Away he bounds, with little fear,
   And seeks the tangled *rough.*

On press his foes, and reach the ground,
   Where's left his half munched meal;
The dogs, in circles, scent around,
   And find his fresh made trail.

With instant cry, away they dash,
   And men as fast pursue;
O'er logs they leap, through water splash,
   And shout the brisk halloo.

Now to elude the eager pack,
   Bear shuns the open ground;
Though matted vines, he shapes his track
   And runs it, round and round.

The tall fleet cur, with deep-mouthed voice,
   Now speeds him, as the wind;
While half-grown pup, and short-legged fice,
   Are yelping far behind.

And fresh recruits are dropping in
   To join the merry *corps:*
With yelp and yell,—a mingled din—
   The woods are in a roar.

And round, and round the chace now goes,
   The world's alive with fun;
Nick Carter's horse, his rider throws,
   And more, Hill drops his gun.

Now sorely pressed, bear glances back,
    And lolls his tired tongue;
When as, to force him from his track,
    An ambush on him sprung.

Across the glade he sweeps for flight,
    And fully is in view.
The dogs, new-fired, by the sight,
    Their cry, and speed, renew.

The foremost ones, now reach his rear,
    He turns, they dash away;
And circling now, the wrathful bear,
    They have him full at bay.

At top of speed, the horse-men come,
    All screaming in a row.
"Whoop! Take him Tiger—Seize him Drum"—
    Bang,—Bang—the rifles go.

And furious now, the dogs he tears,
    And crushes in his ire—
Wheels right and left, and upward rears,
    With eyes of burning fire.

But leaden death is at his heart,
    Vain all the strength he plies—
And, spouting blood from every part,
    He reels, and sinks, and dies.

And now a dinsome clamor rose,
    'Bout who should have his skin;
Who first draws blood, each hunter knows,
    This prize must always win.

But who did this, and how to trace
    What's true from what's a lie,
Like lawyers, in a murder case
    They stoutly *argufy.*

Aforesaid fice, of blustering mood,
    Behind, and quite forgot,
Just now emerging from the wood,
    Arrives upon the spot.

With grinning teeth, and up-turned hair—
    Brim full of spunk and wrath,
He growls, and seizes on dead bear,
    And shakes for life and death.

And swells as if his skin would tear,
    And growls and shakes again;
And swears, as plain as dog can swear,
    That he has won the skin.

Conceited whelp! we laugh at thee—
    Nor mind, that not a few
Of pompous, two-legged dogs there be,
    Conceited quite as you.[29]

4

MAKING HIS WAY
WITH WIT AND WISDOM

1845–1852

As many Whigs split the party to join the new Liberty Party, Lincoln blamed them for Henry Clay's loss in the 1844 presidential race and complained of their insisting on absolute abolition while opposing annexing Texas as extending slavery (Riddle, *Lincoln Runs*, 181; Blue 3-7; Ellsworth 639-40).

3 OCTOBER 1845

I never was much interested in the Texas question. I never could see much good to come of annexation; inasmuch, as they were already a free republican people on our own model; on the other hand, I never could very clearly see how the annexation would augment the evil of slavery. It always seemed to me that slaves would be taken there in about equal numbers, with or without annexation. And if more *were* taken because of annexation, still there would be just so many the fewer left, where they were taken from. It is possibly true, to some extent, that with annexation, some slaves may be sent to Texas and continued in slavery, that otherwise might have been liberated. To whatever extent this may be true, I think annexation an evil. I hold it to be a paramount duty of us in the free states, due to the Union of the states, and perhaps to liberty itself (paradox though it may seem) to let the slavery of the other states alone; while, on the other hand, I hold it to be equally clear, that we should never knowingly lend ourselves directly or indirectly, to prevent that slavery from dying a natural death—to find new places for it to live in, when it can no longer exist in the old. Of course I am not now considering what would be our duty, in cases of insurrection among the slaves.[1]

> In the next year's campaign he was faced with rumors about his religious beliefs circulated by a formidable antagonist, Methodist preacher Peter Cartwright, and asked editors for aid.

AUGUST 1846

I was informed by letter from Jacksonville that Mr. Cartwright was whispering the charge of infidelity against me in that quarter. I at once wrote a contradiction of it, and sent it to my friends there, with the request that they should publish it or not, as in their discretion they might think proper, having in view the extent of the circulation of the charge, as also the extent of credence it might be receiving. They did not publish it. After my return from your part of the District, I was informed that he had been putting the same charge in circulation against me in some of the neighborhoods in our own, and one or two of the adjoining counties. I believe nine persons out of ten had not heard the charge at all; and, in a word, its extent of circulation was just such as to make a public notice of it appear uncalled for; while it was not entirely safe to leave it unnoticed. After some reflection, I published the little hand-bill, herewith enclosed, and sent it to the neighborhoods above referred to.

To the Voters of the Seventh Congressional District.
Fellow Citizens:

A charge having got into circulation in some of the neighborhoods of this District, in substance that I am an open scoffer at *Christianity*, I have by the advice of some friends concluded to notice the subject in this form. That I am not a member of any Christian Church, is true; but I have never denied the truth of the Scriptures; and I have never spoken with intentional disrespect of religion in general, or of any denomination of Christians in particular. It is true that in early life I was inclined to believe in what I understand is called the "Doctrine of Necessity"—that is, that the human mind is impelled to action, or held in rest by some power, over which the mind itself has no control: and I have sometimes (with one, two or three, but never publicly) tried to maintain this opinion in argument—the habit of arguing thus however, I have, entirely left off for more than five years. And I add here, I have always understood this same opinion to be held by several of the Christian denominations. The foregoing, is the whole truth, briefly stated, in relation to myself, upon this subject.

I do not think I could myself, be brought to support a man for office, whom I knew to be an open enemy of, and scoffer at, religion. Leaving the higher matter of eternal consequences, between him and his Maker, I still do not think any man has the right thus to insult the feelings, and injure the morals, of the community in which he may live. If, then, I was guilty of such conduct, I should blame no man who should condemn me for it; but I do blame those, whoever they may be, who falsely put such a charge in circulation against me.[2]

> The rumor was that, while in New Salem, Lincoln had written a tract against the Bible—a rumor Cartwright later found to be false: "I hope," he said, "the good Lord will forgive me from getting any more political bees in my bonnet" (Rankin 284-85). Lincoln carried eight of the eleven counties in the district but still distributed copies of the handbill to quench flareups of the rumor (Riddle, *Lincoln Runs*, 177).

AUGUST 1846

In 1846, he was elected to the lower House of Congress, and served one term only, commencing in Dec. 1847 and ending with the inaugeration of Gen. Taylor, in March 1849.[3]

22 OCTOBER 1846

Being elected to Congress, though I am very grateful to our friends, for having done it, has not pleased me as much as I expected.

We have another boy, born the 10th of March last. He is very much such a child as Bob was at his age—rather of a longer order. Bob is "short and low," and I expect always will be. He talks very plainly,—almost as plainly as any body. He is quite smart enough. I some times fear he is one of the little rare-ripe sort, that are smarter at about five than ever after. He has a great deal of that sort of mischief, that is the offspring of much animal spirits. Since I began this letter a messenger came to tell me, Bob was lost; but by the time I reached the house, his mother had found him, and had him whiped—and, by now, very likely he is run away again.[4]

Saying much more about three-year-old Bob than about baby Eddie, these remarks to Joshua Speed are sometimes taken as evidence of poor parenting, but they seem jocular rather than critical—avoiding, e.g., insensitive allusion to Robert's weak eye (similar to his father's), which would make him appear crosseyed (Burlingame 60-61; Randall 15).

5 DECEMBER 1847

Congress is to organize to-morrow. Last night we held a Whig caucus for the House. The Whig majority in the House is so small that, together with some little dissatis-faction, leaves it doubtful whether we will elect them all.[5]

The Lincolns with the children arrived in Washington 2 December, rooming at Mrs. Ann Spriggs' house, which was favored by anti-slavery Whigs. Amused by his jokes at the dinner table, fellow boarders were nevertheless unnerved by the children, until Mary Lincoln, bored by Washington, took them to her family home in Kentucky. Though Whigs had a majority of four in the 30th Congress, here as in Illinois they were split on abolition and anti-war policy.

8 JANUARY 1848

As to speechmaking, by way of getting the hang of the House, I made a little speech two or three days ago on a post-office question of no general interest. I find speaking here and elsewhere about the same thing. I was about as badly scared, and no worse, as I am when I speak in court. I expect to make one within a week or two, in which I hope to succeed well enough to wish you to see it.

It is very pleasant to me to learn from you that there are some who desire that I should be reelected. I most heartily thank them for the kind partiality, and I can say, as Mr. Clay said of the annexation of Texas, that "personally, I would not object' to a reelection, although I thought at the time, and still think it would be quite as well for me to return to the law at the end of a single term. I made the declaration that I would not be a candidate again, more from a wish to deal fairly with others, to keep peace among our friends, and to keep the district from going to the enemy, than for any cause personal to myself; so that if it should happen that nobody else wishes to be elected I could not refuse the people the right of sending me again. But to enter myself as a competitor of others, or to authorize any one so to enter me, is what my word and honor forbid.[6]

> Overly modest, Lincoln's first speech about distributing mail in the South touched on conflict between government's legislative and executive branches. He erred, however, in leaking the Post Office committee's vote, thus incurring reprimand as recorded in *Congressional Globe* (30th Congress, 1st Session, p. 108 under 5 January 1848). "Intimations were here informally given to Mr. L. that it was not in order to mention on the floor what had taken place in committee. He then observed that if he had been out of order in what he had said, he took it all back, [a laugh] so far as he could. He had no desire, he could assure gentlemen, ever to be out of order—though he never could keep long in order." Such levity endeared him to colleagues. They also laughed at the way he would

stride down the aisles as he spoke, coat-tails flying: "The speech was pretty good," said one, "but I hope he won't charge mileage" (Rice 221).

19 JANUARY 1848

I am kept very busy here; and one thing that perplexes me more than most any thing else, are the cases of whigs calling on me to get them appointments to places in the army, from the President. There are two great obstacles in the way which they do not seem to understand—first, the President has no such appointments to give—and secondly, if he had, he could hardly be expected to give them to whigs, at the solicitation of a whig Member of Congress.[7]

JANUARY 1848

All the battles of the Mexican war had been fought before Mr. L. took his seat in congress, but the American army was still in Mexico, and the treaty of peace was not fully and formally ratified till the June afterwards. Much has been said of his course in Congress in regard to this war. A careful examination of the Journals and Congressional Globe shows, that he voted for all the supply measures which came up, and for all the measures in any way favorable to the officers, soldiers, and their families, who conducted the war through; with this exception that some of the measures passed without yeas and nays, leaving no record as to how particular men voted. The Journals and Globe also show him voting that the war was unnecessarily and unconstitutionally begun by the President of the United States. This is the language of Mr. Ashmun's amendment, for which Mr. L. and nearly or quite all, other whigs of the H.R. voted.

Mr. L's reasons for the opinion expressed by this vote were briefly that the President had sent Genl. Taylor into an inhabited part of the country belonging to Mexico, and not to the U.S. and thereby had provoked the first act of hostility—in fact the commencement of the war; that the place, being the country bordering on the East bank of the Rio Grande, was inhabited by native Mexicans, born there under the Mexican government; and had never submitted to, nor been conquered by Texas, or the U.S. nor transferred to either by treaty—that although Texas claimed the Rio Grande as her boundary, Mexico had never recognized it, the people on the ground had never recognized it, and neither Texas nor the U.S. had ever enforced it—that there was a broad desert between that, and the country over which Texas had actual control—that the country when hostilities commenced, having once belonged to Mexico, must remain so, until it was somehow legally transferred, which had never been done.

Mr. L. thought the act of sending an armed force among the Mexicans, was *unnecessary,* inasmuch as Mexico was in no way molesting, or menacing the U.S. or the people thereof; and that it was *unconstitutional,* because the power of levying war is vested in Congress, and not in the President. He thought the principal motive for the act, was to divert public attention from the surrender of "Fifty-four, forty, or fight" to Great Brittain, on the Oregon boundary question.[8]

> Lincoln was replying to attacks in June 1858 asserting that he had voted against appropriating medical support for the troops in the Mexican War. In that year he would respond in great detail, proving the charges were baseless: they had mistaken the vote of a predecessor, John Henry, against the bill, which passed anyway (*CW* 2:473-74).

I was an old Whig, and whenever the Democratic party tried to get me to vote that the war had been righteously begun by the President, I would not do it. But whenever they asked for any money, or land-warrants, or anything to pay the soldiers there, during all the time, I gave the same vote that Judge Douglas did.[9]

> During the 1858 debates Douglas would refer three times to Lincoln's so-called "Spot Resolutions" insisting on the President's identifying the spot said to have been invaded by Mexico thereby justifying the war. Ten years earlier, Congress had ignored the speech, which merely followed the Whig party line as published eleven days before Lincoln spoke (Riddle, *Congressman*, 33-34).

16 APRIL 1848

Dear Mary:

In this troublesome world, we are never quite satisfied. When you were here, I thought you hindered me some in attending to business; but now, having nothing but business—no variety—it has grown exceedingly tasteless to me. I hate to sit down and direct documents, and I hate to stay in this old room by myself. . . . Suppose you do not prefix the "Hon" to the address on your letters to me any more. I like the letters very much, but I would rather they should not have that upon them. It is not necessary, as I suppose you have thought, to have them to come free. . . . I am afraid you will get so well, and fat, and young, as to be wanting to marry again. What did [Bobby] and Eddie think of the little letters father sent them? Don't let the blessed fellows forget father.[10]

12 JUNE 1848

On my return from Philadelphia, yesterday, where, in my anxiety I had been led to attend the whig convention I found your last letter. . . . The leading matter in your letter, is your wish to return to this side of the Mountains. Will you be a *good girl* in all things, if I consent? Then come along, and that as *soon* as possible. Having got the idea in my head, I shall be impatient till I see you.[11]

> During summer recess the little family toured to Niagara Falls then home to Springfield, where the rest of the family lodged in their old hotel while he returned to work on Zachary Taylor's campaign.

SEPTEMBER 1848

During his term in congress, he advocated Gen. Taylor's nomination for the Presidency, in opposition to all others, and also took an active part for his election, after his nomination—speaking a few times in Maryland, near Washington, several times in Massachusetts, and canvassing quite fully his own district in Illinois, which was followed by a majority in the district of over 1500 for Gen. Taylor.[12]

> His tour of Massachusetts, apparently hoping to emulate Whigs' earlier success in sending Davy Crockett to speak there, was followed by the Illinois tour in October. Taylor won Lincoln's district but failed to carry the state even while winning nationally. At Boston in September Lincoln spoke at Tremont Temple on the program that featured his later secretary of state William H. Seward (Luthin 631).

12 SEPTEMBER 1848

"Mr. L. believed that the self named 'Free Soil' party, was far behind the Whigs. Both parties opposed the extension [of slavery]. As he understood it the new party had no principle except this opposition. If their platform held any other, it was in such a general way that it was like the pair of pantaloons the Yankee pedler offered for sale, 'large enough for any man, small enough for any boy.'"[13]

> His repeated theme was unity on the slavery issue, but he allegedly joked: "With hayseed in my hair, I went to Massachusetts, the most cultured State in the Union, to take a few lessons in deportment" (Herndon & Weik 1:291). To an autograph seeker he was reluctant:

5 JANUARY 1849

I am not a very sentimental man; and the best sentiment I can think of is, that if you collect the signatures of all persons who are no less distinguished than I, you will have a very undistinguishing mass of names.[14]

> Lincoln was having his fun with correspondent C.U. Schlater, who had requested his "signature with a senti-ment" (CW 2:19).

13 JANUARY 1849

Before giving notice to introduce a Bill to abolish slavery in the District of Columbia I visited Mayor, Senators and others whom I thought best acquainted with the sentiment of the people, to ascertain if a Bill such as I proposed would be endorsed by them according to its provisions. Being in-formed by them that it would meet with their hearty approbation I gave notice in Congress that I should introduce a Bill. Subsequently I learned that many southern members of Congress, had been to see the Mayor, and the others who favored my Bill, and had drawn them over to their way of thinking. Finding that I was abandoned by my former backers and having little personal influence, I *dropped* the matter knowing that it was useless to prosecute the business at that time.[15]

> His "bill" was an amendment to Daniel Gott's resolution to abolish the slave trade in the District, which almost drove southerners to walk out. Lincoln's bill was thus an exercise in futility without supporters but consistent with his thinking in March 1837 and 1862.

1849

"The slavery question often bothered me as far back as 1836-40. I was troubled and grieved over it; but after the annexation of Texas I gave it up, believing as I now do, that God will settle it, and settle it right, and that he will, in some inscrutable way, restrict the spread of so great an evil; but for the present it is our duty to wait."[16]

10 MARCH 1849

I, Abraham Lincoln, of Springfield, in the county of Sangamon, in the state of Illinois, have invented a new and improved manner of combining adjustable buoyant air chambers with a steam boat or other vessel for the purpose of enabling their draught of water to be readily lessened to enable them to pass over bars, or through shallow water, without discharging their cargoes.[17]

He supposedly developed the idea returning from

Niagara Falls (with its "mysterious power") on the steamer Globe, October 1848, noting how the captain floated the vessel stuck on a sand bar by using empty casks. The Smithsonian has a model of the invention, which is sketched in *CW* 2:35 (Angle, *Herndon's*, 239-40). It proved too heavy except for flatbottom boats on the shallow waterways of the West.

27 September 1849

I can not but be grateful to you and all other friends who have interested themselves in having the governorship of Oregon offered to me; but on as much reflection as I have had time to give the subject, I cannot consent to accept it.[18]

In return for supporting President Taylor, he had expected the lucrative post of Land Office Commissioner but was offered the governorship of Oregon which would have expired with a Democratic administration in heavily Democratic territory. The appointee in his place, Kentuckian John Pollard Gaines, lost two daughters to yellow fever on the voyage out and had a miserable administration (Miller 391-94; *DAB* s.v. Gaines, John Pollard).

1849

Upon his return from Congress he went to the practice of the law with greater earnestness than ever before.[19]

Principles guiding his practice may be inferred from notes for a lecture intended perhaps for students of the Transylvania University Law Department during his visit to Lexington in late October 1849:

? October 1849

I am not an accomplished lawyer. I find quite as much material for a lecture, in those points wherein I have failed, as in those wherein I have been moderately successful.

The leading rule for the lawyer, as for the man of every calling, is *diligence.* Leave nothing for to-morrow, which can be done to-day. Never let your correspondence fall behind. Whatever piece of business you have in hand, before stopping, do all the labor pertaining to it, which can *then* be done. When you bring a common-law suit, if you have the facts for doing so, write the declaration at once. If a law point be involved, examine the books, and note the authority you rely on, upon the declaration itself, where you are sure to find it when wanted. The same of defences and pleas. In business not likely to be litigated—ordinary collection cases, foreclosures, partitions, and the like,—make all examinations of titles, and note them, and even draft orders and decrees in advance. This course has a tripple advantage; it avoids omissions and neglect, *saves* your labor, when once done; performs the labor out of court when you *have* leisure, rather than in court, when you have not. Extemporaneous speaking should be practiced and cultivated. It is the lawyer's avenue to the public. However able and faithful he may be in other respects, people are slow to bring him business, if he can not make a speech. And yet there is not a more fatal error to young lawyers, than relying too much on speech-making. If any one, upon his rare powers of speaking, shall claim exemption from the drudgery of the law, his case is a failure in advance.

Discourage litigation. Persuade your neighbors to compromise whenever you can. Point out to them how the *nominal* winner is often a *real* loser—in fees, expenses, and waste of time. As a peace-maker the lawyer has a superior opertunity of being a good man. There will still be business enough.

Never stir up litigation. A worse man can scarcely be found than one who does this. Who can be more nearly a fiend than he who habitually overhauls the Register of deeds, in search of defects in titles, whereon to stir up strife, and put money in his pocket? A moral tone ought to be infused into the profession, which should drive such men out of it.

The matter of fees is important far beyond the mere question of bread and butter involved. Properly attended to fuller justice is done to both lawyer and client. An exorbitant fee should never be claimed. As a general rule, never take your whole fee in advance, nor any more than a small retainer. When fully paid before hand, you are more than a common mortal if you can feel the same interest in the case, as if something was still in prospect for you, as well as for your client. And when you lack interest in the case, the job will very likely lack skill and diligence in the performance. Settle the *amount* of fee, and take a note in advance. Then you will feel that you are working for something, and you are sure to do your work faithfully and well. Never sell a fee-note—at least, not before the consideration service is performed. It leads to negligence and dishonesty—negligence by losing interest in the case, and dishonesty in refusing to refund, when you have allowed the consideration to fail.

There is a vague popular belief that lawyers are necessarily dishonest. I say *vague,* because when we consider to what extent *confidence,* and *honors* are reposed in, and conferred upon lawyers by the people, it appears improbable that their *impression* of dishonesty, is very distinct and vivid. Yet the *impression,* is common—almost universal. Let no young man, choosing the law for a calling, for a moment yield to this popular belief. Resolve to be honest at all events; and if, in your own judgment, you can not be an honest-lawyer, resolve to be honest without being a lawyer. Choose some other occupation, rather than one in the choosing of which you do, in advance, consent to be a knave.[20]

> His partner since 1844, William Herndon, concentrated on managing the office and doing research while Lincoln did the litigating.

23 FEBRUARY 1850

We lost our little boy. He was sick fiftytwo days and died the morning of the first day of this month. It was not our *first,* but our second child. We miss him very much.[21]

> Grief at little Eddie's death from pulmonary tuberculosis and Mary's father's death from cholera deepened with the news that Abraham's father was now dying of heart disease.

12 JANUARY 1851

I desire that neither Father or Mother shall be in want of any comfort either in health or sickness while they live. My business is such that I could hardly leave home now, if it were not, as it is, that my own wife is sick-a-bed. (It is a case of baby-sickness, and I suppose is not dangerous.) I sincerely hope Father may yet recover his health; but at all events tell him to remember to call upon, and confide in, our great, and good, and merciful Maker; who will not turn away from him in any extremity. He notes the fall of a sparrow, and numbers the hairs of our heads; and He will not forget the dying man, who puts his trust in Him. Say to him that if we could meet now, it is doubtful whether it would not be more painful than pleasant; but that if it be his lot to go now, he will soon have a joyous [meeting] with many loved ones gone before; and where [the rest] of us, through the help of God, hope ere-long [to join] them.[22]

> At 73, Thomas Lincoln apparently succumbed to a "Seizure of the heart" he had suffered since the previous May. The cold tone of this letter to step-brother John D. Johnston seems understandable considering that Johnston had "cried wolf" earlier, that Mary Lincoln was ill, and that the pietistic message fitted Thomas Lincoln's expectations (Donald 153). Lincoln's love for his stepmother seems to have been reciprocated, for in an 1865 interview she confessed to preferring him to her natural son Johnston (W&D 108). The death of Henry Clay the following year deprived him of a virtual father of his political ideas, evident in Lincoln's eulogy of Clay delivered in Springfield:

5 JULY 1852

Mr. Clays education, to the end of his life, was comparatively limited. I say "to the end of his life," because I have understood that, from time to time, he added something to his education during the greater part of his whole life. Mr. Clay's lack of a more perfect early education, however it may be regretted generally, teaches at least one profitable lesson; it teaches that in this country, one can scarcely be so poor, but that, if he *will*, he *can* acquire sufficient education to get through the world respectably. . . .He ever was, on principle and in feeling, opposed to slavery. The very earliest, and one of the latest public efforts of his life, separated by a period of more than fifty years, were both made in favor of gradual emancipation of the slaves in Kentucky. He did not perceive, that on a question of human right, the negroes were to be excepted from the human race. And yet Mr. Clay was the owner of slaves. Cast into life where slavery was already widely spread and deeply seated, he did not perceive, as I think no wise man has perceived, how it could be at *once* eradicated, without producing a greater evil, even to the cause of human liberty itself. His feeling and his judgment, therefore, ever led him to oppose both extremes of opinion on the subject. Those who would shiver into fragments the Union of these States; tear to tatters its now venerated constitution; and even burn the last copy of the Bible, rather than slavery should continue a single hour, together with all their more halting sympathisers, have received, and are receiving their just execration; and the name, and opinions, and influence of Mr. Clay, are fully, and, as I trust, effectually and enduringly, arrayed against them. But I would also, if I could, array his name, opinions, and influence against the opposite extreme—against a few, but an increasing number of men, who, for the sake of perpetuating slavery, are beginning to assail and to ridicule the white-man's charter of freedom— the declaration that "all men are created free and equal."[23]

> Lincoln considered Clay his "beau ideal of a statesman" (CW 3: 29) and is supposed to have said, "I never had an opinion upon the subject of slavery in my life that I did not get from him" (F2 384). Clay had a much better education than Lincoln implied. He had clerked with celebrated George Wythe and became professor of law at Transylvania University. Lincoln probably meant Clay

lacked classical education (Jones 11). Jones counted "no less than 41 references" or allusions to Clay in the debates with Douglas (21).

14 & 26 AUGUST 1852

Soon after the Democratic nomination for President and Vice-President in June last at Baltimore, it was announced somewhat ostentatiously, as it seemed to me, that Judge Douglas would, previous to the election, make speeches in favor of those nominations, in twenty-eight of the thirty-one States. Since then, and as I suppose, in part performance of this undertaking, he has actually made one speech at Richmond, Virginia. This speech has been published, with high commendations, in at least one of the democratic papers in this State, and I suppose it has been, and will be, in most of the others. When I first saw it, and read it, I was reminded of old times—of the times when Judge Douglas was not so much greater man than all the rest of us, as he now is—of the Harrison campaign, twelve years ago, when I used to hear, and *try* to answer many of his speeches; and believing that the Richmond speech though marked with the same species of "shirks and quirks" as the old ones, was not marked with any greater ability, I was seized with a strong inclination to attempt an answer to it. . . . The new plan or system of tactics is to ridicule and burlesque the whole military character out of credit; and thus to kill Gen. Scott with vexation. Being philosophical and literary men, they have read, and remembered, how the institution of chivalry was ridiculed out of existence by its fictitious votary Don Quixote. They also remember how our own "militia trainings" have been "laughed to death" by fantastic parades and caricatures upon them. We remember one of these parades ourselves here, at the head of which, on horseback, figured our old friend Gordon Abrams, with a pine wood sword, about nine feet long, and a pasteboard cocked hat, from front to rear about the length of an ox yoke, and very much the shape of one turned bottom upwards; and with spurs having rowels as large as the bottom of a teacup, and shanks a foot and a half long. That was the last militia muster here. Among the rules and regulations, no man is to wear more than five pounds of cod-fish for epaulets, or more than thirty pounds of bologna sausages for a sash; and no two men are to dress alike, and if any two should dress alike the one that dresses most alike is to be fined. (I forget how much.) Flags they had too, with devices and mottoes, one of which latter is, "We'll fight till we run, and we'll run till we die." . . . I much doubt if we do not perceive a slight abatement in Judge Douglas' confidence in Providence, as well as in the people. I suspect that confidence is not more firmly fixed with the Judge than it was with the old woman, whose horse ran away with her in a buggy. She said she trusted in Providence till the britchen broke; and then she didn't know what on airth *to* do.[24]

> Lincoln would go on attacking Douglas—four times in the next two months. Douglas had chaired the United States Senate Committee on New Territories and introduced the bill repealing the fragile Missouri Compromise.

5

STUMPING THE STATE AND THE NATION

1854–1860

In 1854, his profession had almost superseded the thought of politics in his mind, when the repeal of the Missouri compromise aroused him as he had never been before.

In the autumn of that year he took the stump with no broader practical aim or object than to secure, if possible, the re-election of Hon Richard Yates to congress. His speeches at once attracted a more marked attention than they had ever before done. As the canvass proceeded, he was drawn to different parts of the state, outside of Mr. Yates' district. He did not abandon the law but gave his attention, by turns, to that and politics.[1]

Whatever the campaign meant to him, Lincoln was particularly anxious "that this Nebraska measure shall be rebuked and condemned every where" (*CW* 2: 228), as in this fragment probably from the speeches he gave during September and October 1854:

SEPTEMBER–OCTOBER 1854?

Although volume upon volume is written to prove slavery

---

a very good thing, we never hear of the man who wishes to take the good of it, *by being a slave himself.*[2]

11 SEPTEMBER 1854

The Kansas and Nebraska territories are now as open to slavery as Mississippi or Arkansas were when they were territories. To illustrate the case—Abraham Lincoln has a fine meadow, containing beautiful springs of water, and well fenced, which John Calhoun had agreed with Abraham (originally owning the land in common) should be his, and the agreement had been consummated in the most solemn manner, regarded by both as sacred. John Calhoun, however, in the course of time, had become owner of an extensive herd of cattle—the prairie grass had become dried up and there was no convenient water to be had. John Calhoun then looks with longing eye on Lincoln's meadow, and goes to it and throws down the fences, and exposes it to the ravages of his starving and famishing cattle. "You rascal," says Lincoln, "what have you done? what do you do this for?"—"Oh," replies Calhoun, "everything is right. I have taken down your fence; but nothing more. It is my true intent and meaning not to drive my cattle into your meadow, nor to exclude them therefrom, but to leave them perfectly free to form their own notions of the feed, and to direct their movements in their own way!"

Now would not the man who committed this outrage be deemed both a knave and a fool,—a knave in removing the restrictive fence, which he had solemnly pledged himself to sustain;—and a fool in supposing that there could be one man found in the country to believe that he had not pulled down the fence for the purpose of opening the meadow for his cattle?[3]

That unsigned editorial in the *Illinois State Journal* referred to a debate with his old friend, now political adversary, John Calhoun. Lincoln thought him a much more formidable debater than Douglas (F2 244).

3 OCTOBER 1854

The State agricultural fair was at Springfield that year, and Douglas was announced to speak there.[4]

Lincoln initiated the tactic of "shadowing" Douglas, replying to his speeches the next day until finally Douglas consented to debate him openly at Peoria. Lincoln's vicious wit surfaces in the concluding image of closing Douglas's mouth with what is now called an infant's pacifier.

16 OCTOBER 1854

The Judge has no very vivid impression that the negro is a human; and consequently has no idea that there can be any moral question in legislating about him. In his view, the question of whether a new country shall be slave or free, is a matter of as utter indifference, as it is whether his neighbor shall plant his farm with tobacco, or stock it with horned cattle. Now, whether this view is right or wrong, it is very certain that the great mass of mankind take a totally different view. They consider slavery a great moral wrong; and their feelings against it, is not evanescent, but eternal. It lies at the very foundation of their sense of justice; and it cannot be trifled with. It is a great and durable element of popular action, and, I think, no statesman can safely disregard it. . . . I think I can answer the Judge so long as he sticks to the premises; but when he flies from them, I can not work an argument into the consistency of a maternal gag, and actually close his mouth with it.[5]

> Lincoln insisted on having as much time on the platform as Douglas had and gave him the closing, feeling confident that the Democrats "would stay for the fun of hearing him skin me" (*CW* 2:247-48). They then all adjourned for two hours, returning at 7 P.M. to hear Douglas skinned for his part in repealing the Missouri Compromise. Energized by such activity, Lincoln put himself forward as candidate for the United States Senate, turning down a seat in the Assembly and on the state Republican Committee, writing to members of the newly seated legislature for their support (D. Fehrenbacher 35).

10 NOVEMBER 1854

Some partial friends are for me for the U.S. Senate; and it would be very foolish, and very false, for me to deny that I would be pleased with an election to that Honorable body.[6]

25 NOVEMBER 1854

I hereby decline to accept the office of Representative in the General Assembly, for the said County of Sangamon, to which office I am reported to have been elected on the 7th of Novr.[7]

19 DECEMBER 1854

I was eight years a representative of Sangamon county in the Legislature; and, although, in a conflict of interests between that and other counties, it perhaps would have been my duty to stick to Old Sangamon; yet it is not within my recollection that the Northern members ever wanted my vote for any interest of theirs, without getting it. . . . As a Senator, I should claim no right, as I should feel no inclination, to give the central portion of the state any preference over the North, or any portion of it.[8]

> A bad snowstorm delayed the contest in the legislature. On the first ballot, Lincoln had five votes short of a majority but since Democrats were rallying to support Governor Joel Matteson, Lincoln retired in favor of antislavery Democrat Lyman Trumbull.

21 FEBRUARY 1855

The election is over, the Session is ended, and I am *not* Senator. I have to content myself with the honor of having been the first choice of a large majority of the fiftyone members who finally made the election. My larger number of friends had to surrender to Trumbull's smaller number, in order to prevent the election of Matteson, which would have been a Douglas victory. . . . A less good humored man than I, perhaps would not have consented to it—and it would not have been done without my consent. I could not, however, let the whole political result go to ruin, on a point merely personal to myself.[9]

24 AUGUST 1855

I think I am a whig; but others say there are no whigs, and that I am an abolitionist. When I was at Washington I voted for the Wilmot Proviso as good as forty times, and I never heard of any one attempting to unwhig me for that. I now do no more than oppose the *extension* of slavery. I am not a Know-Nothing. That is certain. How could I be? How can any one who abhors the oppression of negroes, be in favor of degrading classes of white people? Our progress in degeneracy appears to me to be pretty rapid. As a nation, we began by declaring that *"all men are created equal."* We now practically read it "all men are created equal, *except negroes."* When the Know-Nothings get control, it will read "all men are created equal, except negroes *and foreigners, and catholics."* When it comes to this I should prefer emigrating to some country where they make no pretence of loving liberty—to Russia, for instance, where despotism can be taken pure, and without the base alloy of hypocracy.[10]

> As their party disintegrated, many Whigs drifted to the Know Nothings or new American party until the slavery issue made the new Republican party more attractive, although Lincoln deplored rabid abolitionists as well as exclusionists. Still, he attended the party organizational meeting, where he entertained participants with wit, which more and more he turned upon himself:

22 FEBRUARY 1856

"He felt like the ugly man riding through a wood who met a woman, also on horseback, who stopped and said; 'Well, for land sake you are the homeliest man I ever saw.' 'Yes, madam, but I can't help it,' he replied. 'No, I suppose not,' she observed, 'but you might stay at home.'"[11]

AUGUST–OCTOBER 1856

In the canvass of 1856, Mr. L. made over fifty speeches, no one of which, so far as he remembers, was put in print.[12]

? DECEMBER 1856

Twenty-two years ago Judge Douglas and I first became acquainted. We were both young then; he a trifle younger than I. Even then, we were both ambitious; I, perhaps, quite as much so as he. With *me*, the race of ambition has been a failure—a flat failure; with *him* it has been one of splendid success. His name fills the nation; and is not unknown, even, in foreign lands. I affect no contempt for the high eminence he has reached. So reached, that the oppressed of my species, might have shared with me in the elevation, I would rather stand on that eminence, than wear the richest crown that ever pressed a monarch's brow.[13]

? FEBRUARY 1857

Upon those men who are, in sentiment, opposed to the spread, and nationalization of slavery, rests the task of preventing it. The Republican organization is the embodyment of that sentiment; though, as yet, it by no means embraces all the individuals holding that sentiment. The party is newly formed; and in forming, old party ties had to be broken, and the attractions of party pride, and influential leaders were wholly wanting. In spite of old differences, prejudices, and animosities, it's members were drawn together by a paramount common danger. They formed and manouvered in the face of the deciplined enemy, and in the teeth of all his persistent misrepresentations. Of course, they fell far short of gathering in all of their own. And yet, a year ago, they stood up, an army over thirteen hundred thousand strong. That army is, to-day, the best hope of the nation, and of the world. Their work is before them; and from which they may not guiltlessly turn away.[14]

As an architect of the party in Illinois, Lincoln remained optimistic about results of the 1856 election. Unsuccessfully put up as vice-presidential nominee, he easily saw how the American Party would siphon votes from Republican candidate John C. Fremont and ensure victory for James Buchanan as president. But he also saw that Buchanan would have been beaten by a united front; and, further, Republicans elected a governor in Illinois. Though now devoting more time to his legal practice, Lincoln still took to the platform after Douglas:

26 JUNE 1857

He finds the Republicans insisting that the Declaration of Independence includes ALL men, black as well as white; and forthwith he boldly denies that it includes negroes at all, and proceeds to argue gravely that all who contend it does, do so only because they want to vote, and eat, and sleep, and marry with negroes! He will have it that they cannot be consistent else. Now I protest against that counterfeit logic which concludes that, because I do not want a black woman for a *slave* I must necessarily want her for a *wife*. I need not have her for either, I can just leave her alone. In some respects she certainly is not my equal; but in her natural right to eat the bread she earns with her own hands without asking leave of any one else, she is my equal, and the equal of all others.[15]

18 MAY 1858?

A House divided against itself cannot stand. I believe the government cannot endure permanently half slave and half free. I expressed this belief a year ago; and subsequent developments have but confirmed me. I do not expect the Union to be dissolved. I do not expect the house to fall; but I do expect it will cease to be divided. It will become all one thing or all the other. Either the opponents of slavery will arrest the further spread of it, and put it in course of ultimate extinction; or its advocates will push it forward till it shall become alike lawful in all the States, old as well as new.

> Every schoolboy would have been familiar with the house-divided image from the Bible or from Daniel Webster's reply to Robert Hayne, a staple in textbooks. Lincoln had used it with reference to Whig unity in 1843 and to slavery's effect on the nation in 1855. He now referred to the Supreme Court's Dred Scott decision, probably in notes for the speech accepting the Republican nomination for Senator against Douglas. Some editors claimed to be puzzled by the statement:

23 June 1858

I have declared a thousand times, and now repeat that, in my opinion, neither the General Government, nor any other power outside of the slave states, can constitutionally or rightfully interfere with slaves or slavery where it already exists. I believe that whenever the effort to spread slavery into the new teritories, by whatever means, and into the free states themselves, by Supreme court decisions, shall be fairly headed off, the institution will then be in course of ultimate extinction; and by the language used I meant only this.[17]

> Besides familiar allusions, Lincoln also relied on historical traditions. In this next instance—intended or not—he echoes George Washington's address to mutinous troops,

Newburgh 1783, when the General paused, took out his spectacles, and apologized for the pause: "Observing at the same time, that he had grown gray in their service, and now found himself growing blind" (Shaw 104).

10 JULY 1858

Reading from speeches is a very tedious business, particularly for an old man that has to put on spectacles, and the more so if the man be so tall that he has to bend over to the light. . . .

Judge Douglas informed you that this speech of mine was probably carefully prepared. I admit that it was. I am not master of language; I have not a fine education; I am not capable of entering into a disquisition upon dialectics, as I believe you call it; but I do not believe the language I employed bears any such construction as Judge Douglas put upon it. But I don't care about a quibble in regard to words. I know what I meant. . . .

I do not claim, gentlemen, to be unselfish, I do not pretend that I would not like to go to the United States Senate, I make no such hypocritical pretense, but I do say to you that in this mighty issue, it is nothing to you—nothing to the mass of the people of the nation, whether or not Judge Douglas or myself shall ever be heard of after this night, it may be a trifle to either of us, but in connection with this mighty question, upon which hang the destinies of the nation, perhaps, it is absolutely nothing.[18]

17 JULY 1858

Senator Douglas is of world wide renown. All the anxious politicians of his party, or who have been of his party for years past, have been looking upon him as certainly, at no distant day, to be the President of the United States. They have seen in his round, jolly, fruitful face, postoffices, landoffices, marshalships, and cabinet appointments, chargeships and foreign missions, bursting and sprouting out in wonderful exuberance ready to be laid hold of by their greedy hands. And as they have been gazing upon this attractive picture so long, they cannot, in the little distraction that has taken place in the party, bring themselves to give up the charming hope; but with greedier anxiety they rush about him, sustain him, and give him marches, triumphal entries, and receptions beyond what even in the days of his highest prosperity they could have brought about in his favor. On the contrary nobody has ever expected me to be President. In my poor, lean, lank, face, nobody has ever seen that any cabbages were sprouting out.[19]

> Douglas interrupted a state-wide tour to reply to that attack, finally conceding to a series of formal debates between June and November across the state, during which Lincoln would make over sixty speeches. After the debate at Ottawa, 21 August, Douglas's supporters carried him on their shoulders in triumph. When Lincoln's supporters tried to do the same, he insisted, "Don't, don't! This is ridiculous" (Ward 200).

1 AUGUST 1858?

As I would not be a *slave*, so I would not be a *master*. This expresses my idea of democracy. Whatever differs from this, to the extent of the difference, is no democracy.[20]

30 OCTOBER 1858

To-day closes the discussions of this canvass. The planting and the culture are over; and there remains but the preparation, and the harvest. I stand here surrounded by friends—some *political, all personal* friends, I trust. May I be indulged, in this closing scene, to say a few words of myself. I have borne a laborious, and, in some respects to myself, a painful part in the contest. Through all, I have neither assailed, nor wrestled with any part of the Constitution. The legal right of the Southern people to reclaim their fugitives I have constantly admitted. The legal right of Congress to interfere with their institution in the states, I have constantly denied. In resisting the spread of slavery to new territory, and with that, what appears to me to be a tendency to subvert the first principle of free government itself my whole effort has consisted. To the best of my judgment I have labored *for,* and not *against* the Union. As I have not felt, so I have not expressed any harsh sentiment towards our Southern bretheren. I have constantly declared, as I really believed, the only difference between them and us, is the difference of circumstances.

I have meant to assail the motives of no party, or individual; and if I have, in any instance (of which I am not conscious) departed from my purpose, I regret it.

I have said that in some respects the contest has been painful to me. Myself, and those with whom I act have been constantly accused of a purpose to destroy the Union; and bespattered with every immaginable odious epithet; and some who were friends, as it were but yesterday have made themselves most active in this. I have cultivated patience, and made no attempt at a retort.

Ambition has been ascribed to me. God knows how

sincerely I prayed from the first that this field of ambition might not be opened. I claim no insensibility to political honors; but today could the Missouri restriction be restored, and the whole slavery question replaced on the old ground of "toleration by *necessity* where it exists," with unyielding hostility to the spread of it, on principle, I would, in consideration, gladly agree, that Judge Douglas should never be *out*, and I never *in*, an office, so long as we both or either, live.[21]

2 November 1858

"The evening of the day in 1858, that decided the contest for the Senate between Mr. Douglas and myself, was dark, rainy and gloomy. I had been reading the returns, and had ascertained that we had lost the Legislature and started to go home. The path had been worn hog-backed and was slippering. My foot slipped from under me, knocking the other one out of the way, but I recovered myself and lit square: and I said to myself, *'It's a slip and not a fall.'*"[22]

Prefaced by a remark about being "pretty sure-footed," Lincoln reminisced in wrestling terms during conversation; while in letters he reassured followers, "The fight must go on" and "I think we have fairly entered upon a durable struggle as to whether this nation is to be ultimately become all slave or all free" and even, "Another 'blow-up' is coming; and we shall have fun again" (*CW* 3:340, 342, 344). His party had won the popular vote but Democrats had 53 percent of seats in the state senate where Douglas was chosen.

19 NOVEMBER 1858

I am glad I made the late race. It gave me a hearing on the great and durable question of the age, which I could have had in no other way; and though I now sink out of view, and shall be forgotten, I believe I have made some marks which will tell for the cause of Civil liberty long after I am gone.[23]

> Responding to a proposal that he publish his speeches made during the Douglas debates, Lincoln offered a counterproposal that eventually resulted in a book funded by the Republican party but executed by Lincoln himself. Within months of publication, Spring 1860, more than 30,000 copies were sold by publisher Follett, Foster, and Company. Lincoln received 100 copies. The book, priced at $1.00, had 268 pages of packed print.

26 MARCH 1859

I would really be pleased with a publication substantially as [proposed]. But I would suggest a few variations from your plan. I would not include the Republican platform; because that would give the work a one-sided and party cast, unless the democratic platform was also included.

I would not take *all* the speeches from the Press & Tribune; but I would take mine from that paper; and those of Judge Douglas from the Chicago Times. This would represent each of us, as reported by his own friends, and thus be mutual, and fair. I would take the speeches alone; rigidly excluding all comments of the newspapers.

I would include the correspondence between Judge Douglas and myself which led to the joint discussions.

I would call the thing "Illinois political canvass of

1858"; and, as falling within the title, I would select and include half a dozen of the National Democratic speeches.

Last autumn and winter I got up a Scrap-book precisely on the plan I have stated. The parts stand in the order following—

My speech at Springfield, at the Republican convention, June 16, 1858.

Douglas' speech at Chicago, July 9, 1858

My speech at Chicago, July 10, 1858.

Douglas' speech at Bloomington July 16, 1858

Douglas' speech at Springfield, July 17, 1858

My speech at Springfield, July 17, 1858—

The correspondence which led to the joint discussions.

The joint discussions, in the order in which they occurred.

The National Democratic speeches, to come in after the others, in the order among themselves in which they were delivered.

In my own speeches I have corrected only a few small typographical errors. The other speeches I have not touched; but merely pasted them in from the papers in which they were reported.

Judge Douglas would have the right to correct typographical errors in his, if he desired; but I think the necessity, in his case, would be less than in mine; because he had two hired reporters travelling with him, and probably revised their manuscripts before they went to press; while I had no reporter of my own, but depended on a very excellent one sent by the Press & Tribune; but who never waited to show me his notes or manuscripts; so that the first I saw of my speeches, after delivering them, was in the Press & Tribune precisely as they now stand.

My Scrap-book would be the best thing to print from;

still, as it cost me a good deal of labor to get it up, and as I am very desirous to preserve the substance of it permanently, I would not let it go out of my own control. If an arrangement could be made to print it in Springfield, under my own supervision, I would allow the Scrap-book to be used, and would claim no share in any profit that could be made out of the publication.[24]

> The debates with Douglas reprinted in the press as well as the book made a strong impression across the nation. Turning down an invitation to speak in Boston on Jefferson's birthday, Lincoln summed up his position, "He who would *be* no slave, must consent to *have* no slave," and his attitude toward party labels:

6 APRIL 1859

The democracy of to-day hold the *liberty* of one man to be absolutely nothing, when in conflict with another man's right of *property*. Republicans, on the contrary, are for both the *man* and the *dollar;* but in cases of conflict, the man *before* the dollar.

I remember once being much amused at seeing two partially intoxicated men engage in a fight with their greatcoats on, which fight, after a long, and rather harmless contest, ended in each having fought himself out of his own coat, and *into* that of the other. If the two leading parties of this day are really identical with the two in the days of Jefferson and Adams, they have performed about the same feat as the two drunken men.[25]

> At home he was being mentioned for the presidency while invitations from Ohio gave him the chance to elaborate on his debates with Douglas:

16 APRIL 1859

I must, in candor, say I do not think myself fit for the Presidency. I certainly am flattered and gratified that some partial friends think of me in that connection; but I really think it best for our case that no concerted effort should be made.[26]

> In Cincinnati he argued that slave labor devalues labor of freemen and thus obstructs an industrious worker's progress toward such success as he himself had achieved.

17 SEPTEMBER 1859

The assumption that the slave is in a better condition than the hired laborer, includes the further assumption that he who is once a hired laborer always remains a hired laborer; that there is a certain class of men who remain through life in a dependent condition. Then they endeavor to point out that when they get old they have no kind masters to take care of them, and that they fall dead in the traces, with the harness of actual labor upon their feeble backs. In point of fact that is a false assumption. There is no such thing as a man who is a hired laborer, of a necessity, always remaining in his early condition. The general rule is otherwise. I know it is so, and I will tell you why.

When at an early age, I was myself a hired laborer, at twelve dollars per month; and therefore I do know that there is not always the necessity for actual labor because once there was propriety in being so. My understanding of the hired laborer is this: A young man finds himself of an age to be dismissed from parental control; he has for his capital nothing save two strong hands that God has given him, a heart willing to labor, and a freedom to choose the mode of his work and the manner of his employer; he has got no soil nor shop, and he avails himself of the opportunity of hiring himself to some man who has capital to pay him a fair day's wages for a fair day's work. He is benefited by availing himself of that privilege. He works industriously, he behaves soberly, and the result of a year or two's labor is a surplus of capital. Now he buys land on his own hook; he settles, marries, begets sons and daughters, and in course of time he too has enough capital to hire some new beginner. . . . This progress by which the poor, honest, industrious, and resolute man raises himself, that he may work on his own account, and hire somebody else, is that progress that human nature is entitled to, is that improvement in condition that is intended to be secured by those institutions under which we live, is the great principle for which this government was really formed. Our government was not established that one man might do with himself as he pleases, and with another man too.

I hold that if there is any one thing that can be proved to be the will of God by external nature around us, without reference to revelation, it is the proposition that whatever any one man earns with his hands and by the sweat of his brow, he shall enjoy in peace. I say that whereas God Almighty has given every man one mouth to be fed, and one pair of hands adapted to furnish food for that mouth, if anything can be proved to be the will of Heaven, it is proved by this fact, that that mouth is to be fed by those hands, without being interfered with by any other man who has also his mouth to feed and his hands to labor with. I hold if the Almighty had ever made a set of men that should do all the eating and none of the work, he would have made them with mouths only and no hands, and if had ever made another class that he had intended should do all the work and none of the eating, he would have made them without mouths and with all hands.[27]

> In supplying personal data for eastern editors, he said, "There is not much of it, for the reason, I suppose, that there is not much of me" (*CW* 3:511). New Yorkers must have felt otherwise, for they invited him to speak at Brooklyn's celebrated Plymouth Church. On arriving in February, he found that the meeting would be a symposium on abolition at Cooper Institute before a distinguished audience, including William Cullen Bryant and Horace Greeley, along with members of the foreign and national press. His well reasoned explanation of principles concluded:

27 February 1860

Let us stand by our duty, fearlessly and effectively. Let us be diverted by none of those sophistical contrivances wherewith we are so industriously plied and belabored—contrivances such as groping for some middle ground between the right and the wrong, vain as the search for a man who should be neither a living man nor a dead man—such as a policy of "don't care" on a question about which all true men do care—such as Union appeals beseeching true Union men to yield to Disunionists, reversing the divine rule, and calling, not the sinners, but the righteous to repentance—such as invocations to Washington, imploring men to unsay what Washington said, and undo what Washington did.

Neither let us be slandered from our duty by false accusations against us, nor frightened from it by menaces of destruction to the Government, nor of dungeons to ourselves. Let us have faith that right makes might, and in that

faith, let us, to the end, dare to do our duty, as we understand it.[28]

His growing popularity in the East meant adding toil to a
planned visit with son Robert at Phillips Exeter Academy
near Boston.

4 MARCH 1860

If I had foreseen it I think I would not have come East at all.
The speech at New York, being within my calculations before I started, went off passably well, and gave me no trouble
whatever. The difficulty was to make nine others, before
reading audiences, who had already seen all my ideas in
print.[29]

Taking encouragement from his successful tour of the
East Coast, he began to reconsider the increasing number
of suggestions that he run for president, but he did not
wish to interfere with others' plans.

24 MARCH 1860

If I have any chance, it consists mainly in the fact that the
whole opposition would vote for me if nominated. (I don't
mean to include the pro-slavery opposition of the South,
of course.) My name is new in the field; and I suppose I
am not the *first* choice of a very great many. Our policy,
then, is to give no offence to others—leave them in a
mood to come to us, if they shall be compelled to give
up their first love. This, too, is dealing justly with all, and
leaving us in a mood to support heartily whoever shall be
nominated.[30]

6 April 1860

Remembering that when a not very great man, begins to be mentioned for a very great position, his head is very likely to be a little turned, I conclude I am not the fittest person to answer the questions [of best Republican presidential prospect].[31]

> Cornelius McNeill, editor of the *Iroquois Republican,* heard rumors that Lincoln had been paid $200 to make the Cooper Institute speech rather than merely to cover expenses. For contrast, Lincoln's supporters spent $321.50 entertaining national convention delegates while the party raised some $12,500 for the national campaign (Pratt, *Personal,* 108-12).

6 April 1860

Last October I was requested, by letter, to deliver some sort of speech in Mr. Beecher's church, in Brooklyn, $200 being offered in the first letter. I wrote that I could do it in February, provided they would take a political speech, if I could find time to get up no other. They agreed, and subsequently I informed them the speech would have to be a political one. When I reached New York, I, for the first, learned that the place was changed to "Cooper Institute." I made the speech, and left for New Hampshire, where I have a son at school, neither asking for pay nor having any offered me. Three days after, a check for $200 was sent to me, at N.H., and I took it, *and did not know it was wrong.* My understanding now is, though I knew nothing of it at the time, that they did charge for admittance, at the Cooper Institute, and that they took in more than twice $200.[32]

7 APRIL 1860

I am not a professional lecturer. Have never got up but one lecture, and that I think rather a poor one. Besides, what time I can spare from my own business this season I shall be compelled to give to politics.[33]

29 APRIL 1860

I will be entirely frank. The taste *is* in my mouth a little; and this, no doubt, disqualifies me, to some extent, to form correct opinions.[34]

> In this limited disqualification, Lincoln again asserted a willingness to run but not at the expense of splitting the party, at that time weakened by feuds among supporters of William Henry Seward, Salmon P. Chase, and Edward Bates, each of whom would eventually be enfolded in Lincoln's cabinet. Illinois Republicans named him unanimous choice as national candidate, calling him nostalgically "Rail Splitter," after his cousin carried through the convention a rail Abe was supposed to have split. Rails thereafter became an icon of the campaign.

9 MAY 1860

"I don't know whether we made those rails or not. Fact is, I don't think they are a Credit to the Makers."[35]

> At the Chicago national convention he was nominated on the third ballot. Legend has it that, notified by wire in Springfield, he is supposed to have postponed celebrating: "There is a little woman at our house who is probably more interested in this dispatch than I am" (W&D 491). One penalty of playing on a broader stage was extension

of the range of misunderstanding and misinterpretation even of words uttered in jest.

16 AUGUST 1860

Soon after the Chicago nomination I was written to by a highly respectable gentleman of Hardin County, Ky, inquiring if I was a son of Thomas Lincoln, whom he had known long ago, in that county. I answered that I was, and that I was myself born there. He wrote again, and, among other things, (did not *invite* me but) simply *inquired* if it would not be agreeable to me to revisit the scenes of my childhood. I replied, among other things, "It would indeed, but would you not Lynch me?" He did not write again. I have, *playfully,* (and never otherwise) related this incident several times.[36]

> Anxious about Kentuckians misunderstanding the fun letter, he composed that "correction" to counter Democratic slander circulating in the state. At the same time, he was called upon to supply graphic images:

13 SEPTEMBER 1860

The original of the picture was taken from life, and is, *I* think, a very true one; though my wife, and many others, do not. My impression is that their objection arises from the disordered condition of the hair. My judgment is worth nothing in these matters. If your friend could procure one of the "heads" "busts" or whatever you call it, by Volk at Chicago, I should think it the thing for him.[37]

> The photograph referred to was made by Alexander Hesler (Meserve 6) and the bust by Leonard Volk in late March or April 1860. Volk made the bust before Lincoln

grew a beard, supposed to have been inspired by eleven-year-old Grace Bedell, whose letter received wide press coverage. Of the bust, Lincoln is supposed to have remarked, "There was the animal himself!" (L.W. Volk, "The Lincoln Life-Mask and How It Was Made," *Century* 23 [December 1881], 228). To Grace Bedell, he responded in a letter of October 19.

19 OCTOBER 1860

I regret the necessity of saying I have no daughters. I have three sons—one seventeen, one nine, and one seven, years of age. . . . As to the whiskers, having never worn any, do you not think people would call it a piece of silly affectation if I were to begin it now?[38]

The next February on his way to Washington, Lincoln stopped at a station just outside Erie, Pennsylvania, made his way through the crowd to find "I think her name was Miss Barlly," and when a little boy pointed her out, implanted "several hearty kisses" (*NY Tribune,* 18 February 1861). During the campaign, however, his managers restricted public appearances, instead encouraged young voters to form "Wide Awake" clubs to promote his election.

25 OCTOBER 1860

"For personal considerations, I would rather have a full term in the Senate—a place in which I would feel more consciously able to discharge the duties required and where there was more chance to make reputation and less danger of losing it—than four years of the presidency."[39]

27 October 1860

What is it I could say which would quiet alarm? Is it that no interference by the government, with slaves or slavery within the states, is intended? I have said this so often already, that a repetition of it is but mockery, bearing an appearance of weakness, and cowardice, which perhaps should be avoided. Why do not uneasy men *read* what I have already said? and what our *platform* says?[40]

Despite Republican successes in off-year elections nationally, he remained pessimistic about his chances. The campaign split the Democrats between candidates Douglas and southerner J.C. Breckenridge, with minor-party candidate John Bell making it a four-man race. Although Lincoln garnered only 40 percent of the popular vote, he was able to enjoy a comfortable margin in the electoral college, thus becoming the first Republican president.

6

PRESERVING, PROTECTING, DEFENDING

1860–1863

South Carolina, disdaining the election results, seceded from the Union on 20 December. When Lincoln heard rumors that President Buchanan had surrendered a fort there, he said, "If that is true, they ought to hang him" (F2 343). But pressures of trying to preserve the nation from dissolving may be seen in near-mystical experiences Lincoln is said to have had:

7 NOVEMBER 1860

"It was just after my election in 1860, when the news had been coming in thick and fast all day, and there had been a great 'Hurrah, boys!' so that I was all tired out, and went home to rest, throwing myself down on a lounge in my chamber. Opposite where I lay was a bureau, with a swinging-glass upon it and, looking in that glass, I saw myself reflected, nearly at full length; but my face, I noticed, had *two* separate and distinct images, the tip of the nose of one being about three inches from the tip of the other. I was a little bothered, perhaps startled, and got up and looked in the glass, but the illusion vanished. On lying down again I saw it a second time—plainer, if possible, than before; and then I noticed that one of the faces was a little paler, say five shades, than the other. I got up and the thing melted away, and I went off and, in the excitement of the hour, forgot all about it—nearly, but not quite, for the thing would once in a while come up, and give me a little pang, as though something uncomfortable had happened. When I went home I told my wife about it, and a few days after, I tried the experiment again, when, sure enough, the thing came again; but I never succeeded in bringing the ghost back after that, though I once tried very industriously to show it to my wife, who was worried about it somewhat. She thought it was 'a sign' that I was to be elected to a second term of office, and that the paleness of one of the faces was an omen that I should not see life through the last term. . . . If they kill me, the next man will be just as bad for them; and in a country like this, where our habits are simple, and must be, assassination is always possible, and will come if they are determined upon it."[1]

15 NOVEMBER 1860

The ugly point is the necessity of keeping the government together by force, as ours should be a government of fraternity.[2]

WINTER 1860–1861

"Of all the trials I have had since I came here, none begin to compare with those I had between the inauguration and the fall of Fort Sumter. They were so great that could I have anticipated them, I would not have believed it possible to survive them."[3]

As Lincoln prepared his inaugural address, six of seven states that had seceded formed the Confederate States of America (Texas was the exception). Before leaving Springfield for the national capitol, he had copies of his draft printed with broad margins for comments by colleagues.

2 FEBRUARY 1861

I have the document already blocked out; but in the now rapidly shifting scenes, I shall have to hold it subject to revision up to near the time of delivery.[4]

He left Springfield on 11 February with a poignant farewell address:

11 FEBRUARY 1861

My friends—No one, not in my situation, can appreciate my feeling of sadness, at this parting. To this place, and the kindness of these people, I owe every thing. Here I have lived a quarter of a century, and have passed from a young to an old man. Here my children have been born, and one is buried. I now leave, not knowing when, or whether ever, I may return, with a task before me greater than that which rested upon Washington. Without the assistance of that Divine Being, who ever attended him, I cannot succeed. With that assistance I cannot fail. Trusting in Him, who can go with me, and remain with you and be every where for good, let us confidently hope that all will yet be well. To His care commending you, as I hope in your prayers you will commend me, I bid you an affectionate farewell.[5]

The trip by rail to Washington took twelve days because of obligatory whistle stops and formal speeches in major cities along the way:

11 FEBRUARY 1861

(Lafayette, Indiana) We have seen great changes within the recollection of some of us who are the older. When I first came to the west, some 44 or 45 years ago, at sundown you had completed a journey of some 30 miles which you had commenced at sunrise, and thought you had done well. Now only six hours have elapsed since I left my home in Illinois where I was surrounded by a large concourse of my fellow citizens, almost all of whom I could recognize, and I find myself far from home surrounded by the thousands I now see before me, who are strangers to me. Still we are bound together, I trust in christianity, civilization and patriotism, and are attached to our country and our whole country. While some of us may differ in political opinions, still we are all united in one feeling for the Union. . . . and permit me to express the sentiment that upon the union of the States, there shall be between us no difference.[6]

The Republican newspapers covered the trip in detail, sometimes—in the New York *Tribune*—capturing the interplay between President-elect and people:

19 FEBRUARY 1861

(New York City) I have been occupying the position, since the election, of silence—of avoiding public speaking. I have been doing so because I thought, upon due consideration, that was the proper course for me to take. (Applause.) I am brought before you now to make a speech, while you all approve, more than anything else, that I have been keeping silence. (Great laughter and renewed cheering, the audience taking the full humor of the thing.) It seems to me the response you give to that remark ought to justify me in closing just here. (More laughter.) I had not kept silence since the Presidential Election from any party craftiness or for any indifference to the anxieties that pervade the minds of men in this country. I have kept silence for that it was peculiarly proper for me to wait until the time should come when, according to the custom of the country, I would speak officially. (Voice, partially interrogative, partially sarcastic, "Custom of the country?") I allude to the custom of the Presidents taking the oath of office, of his declaring what course he thinks should be pursued. That is what I mean.[7]

22 February 1861

(Independence Hall, Philadelphia) I am filled with deep emotion at finding myself standing here, in this place, where were collected together the wisdom, the patriotism, the devotion to principle, from which sprang the institutions under which we live. You have kindly suggested to me that in my hands is the task of restoring peace to the present distracted condition of the country. I can say in return that all the political sentiments I entertain have been drawn, so far as I have been able to draw them, from the sentiments which originated, and were given to the world from this hall. I have never had a feeling politically that did not spring from the sentiments embodied in the Declaration of Independence. I have often pondered over the dangers which were incurred by the men who assembled here, and framed and adopted that Declaration of Independence.

I have pondered over the toils that were endured by the officers and soldiers of the army who achieved that Independence. I have often inquired of myself what great principle or idea it was that kept this Confederacy so long together. It was not the mere matter of the separation of the Colonies from the mother land; but that sentiment in the Declaration of Independence which gave liberty, not alone to the people of this country, but, I hope, to the world for all future time. It was that which gave promise that in due time the weight would be lifted from the shoulders of all men. This is a sentiment embodied in that Declaration of Independence. Now, my friends, can this country be saved upon that basis? If it can, I will consider myself one of the happiest men in the world if I can help to save it. If it can not be saved upon that principle, it will be truly awful. But if this country can not be saved without giving up that principle, I was about to say I would rather be assassinated on this spot than surrender it. . . . My friends, this is wholly an unexpected speech, and I did not expect to be called upon to say a word when I came here. I supposed it was merely to do something toward raising the flag. I may, therefore, have said something indiscreet. I have said nothing but what I am willing to live by and, if it be the pleasure of Almighty God, die by.[8]

> The allusion to assassination and death could have referred to rumors that conspirators planned to kill him as his train made a stop at Baltimore, as reported to him by both military sources and Allan Pinkerton's detectives. Officials rescheduled the train.

21 FEBRUARY 1861

"There were stories or rumors some time ago, before I left

home, about people who were intending to do me a mischief. I never attached much importance to them—never wanted to believe any such thing. So I never would do any thing about them, in the way of taking precautions and the like. Some of my friends, though, thought differently and, without my knowledge, they employed a detective to look into the matter. He brought this story, or something similar to it, about an attempt on my life in the confusion and hurly-burly of the reception at Baltimore."[9]

28 FEBRUARY 1861

I have reached this city of Washington under circumstances considerably differing from those under which any other man has ever reached it. I have reached it for the purpose of taking an official position amongst the people, almost all of whom were opposed to me, and are yet opposed to me, as I suppose. I thought much of the ill feeling that has existed between you and the people of your surroundings and that people from amongst whom I come, has depended, and now depends, upon a misunderstanding. I hope that if things shall go along as prosperously as I believe we all desire they may, I may have it in my power to remove something of this misunderstanding—that I may be enabled to convince you, and the people of your section of the country, that we regard you as in all things being our equals—in all things entitled to the same respect and to the same treatment that we claim for ourselves—that we are in no wise disposed, if it were in our power, to oppress you or deprive you of any of your rights under the constitution of the United States or even narrowly to split hairs with you in regard to these rights. But are determined to give you, so far as lies in our hands, all your rights under the constitution, not grudgingly, but fully and fairly. I hope that by thus dealing with you we will become better acquainted and be better friends.[10]

FEBRUARY 1861

"It seems to me that Douglas got the best of it at the election last fall. I am left to face an empty treasury and a great rebellion, while my own party endorses his popular sovereignty idea, and applies it in legislation."[11]

> Among the revisions suggested by friends, the ringing conclusion of the inaugural address adopts phrases proposed by Secretary of State William H. Seward (*CW* 4:271; HM 235844; LC film frame 7744).

4 MARCH 1861

In *your* hands, my dissatisfied fellow countrymen, and not in *mine,* is the momentous issue of the civil war. The government will not assail *you,* unless you *first* assail *it.* You can have no conflict without being yourselves the aggressors. *You* have no oath registered in Heaven to destroy the government, while *I* shall have the most solemn one to "preserve, protect, and defend" it. *You* can forbear the *assault* upon it; *I* can *not* shrink from the *defense* of it. With *you,* and not with *me,* is the solemn question of "Shall it be peace, or a sword?"

I am loth to close. We are not enemies, but friends. We must not be enemies. Though passion may have strained, it must not break our bonds of affection. The mystic chords of memory, streching from every battlefield, and patriot grave, to every living heart and hearthstone, all over this broad land, will yet swell the chorus of the Union, when again touched, as surely they will be, by the better angels of our nature.[12]

> To a special session of Congress, Lincoln justified using "the warpower" of his office, viewing the Confederacy not as a rebellion but as an insurrection by dissatisfied citizens who needed reformation.

4 July 1861

This issue embraces more than the fate of these United States. It presents to the whole family of man, the question whether a democracy—a government of the people, by the same people—can, or can not, maintain it's territorial integrity, against it's own domestic foes. It presents the question, whether discontented individuals, too few in numbers to control administration, according to organic law, in any case, can always, upon the pretences made in this case, or on any other pretences, or arbitrarily, without any pretence, break up their Government, and thus practically put an end to free government upon the earth. It forces us to ask: "Is there, in all republics, this inherent, and fatal weakness?" "Must a government, of necessity, be too *strong* for the liberties of it's own people, or too *weak* to maintain it's own existence?" So viewing the issue, the administration had no choice left but to call out the military power of the Government; and so to resist force employed for it's destruction, by force for it's preservation.[13]

Spring 1861

"I am like a man so busy in letting rooms in one end of his house, that he can't stop to put out the fire that is burning the other."[14]

General John C. Fremont published a proclamation confiscating slaves of Missourians partial to the Confederacy. After repeated reprimands, Lincoln replaced him, insisting that neither general nor president "may make permanent rules of property by proclamation," the purview of the legislature (*CW* 4:532).

22 September 1861

Genl. Fremont's proclamation as to confiscation of property, and the liberation of slaves, is *purely political,* and not within the range of *military* law. . . . The proclamation in the point in question, is simply "dictatorship." It assumes that the general may do *anything* he pleases—confiscate the lands and free the slaves of *loyal* people, as well as of disloyal ones. And going the whole figure I have no doubt would be more popular with some thoughtless people, than that which has been done! But I can not assume this reckless position; nor allow others to assume it on my responsibility.[15]

29 September 1861

I am compelled to watch all points. While I write this I am, if not in *range,* at least in *hearing* of cannon-shot, from an army of enemies more than a hundred thousand strong. I do not expect them to capture this city; but I *know* they would, if I were to send the men and arms from here, to defend Louisville, of which there is not a single hostile armed soldier within forty miles, nor any force known to be moving upon it from any distance.[16]

Besides domestic pressures, the President faced such problems as keeping cotton-consumer England from supporting the Confederacy. In his message to Congress he discussed broad issues, concluding with a restatement of economic principles based on his own experience.

3 DECEMBER 1861

There is one point, with its connexions, not so hackneyed as most others, to which I ask a brief attention. It is the effort to place *capital* on an equal footing with, if not above *labor,* in the structure of government. It is assumed that labor is available only in connexion with capital; that nobody labors unless somebody else, owning capital, somehow by the use of it, induces him to labor. This assumed, it is next considered whether it is best that capital shall *hire* laborers, and thus induce them to work by their own consent, or *buy* them, and drive them to it without their consent. Having proceeded so far, it is naturally concluded that all laborers are either *hired* laborers, or what we call slaves. And further, it is assumed that whoever is once a hired laborer, is fixed in that condition for life.

Now, there is no such relation between capital and labor as assumed; nor is there any such thing as a free man being fixed for life in the condition of a hired laborer. . . . There is not, of necessity any such thing as the free hired laborer being fixed to that condition for life. Many independent men everywhere in these States, a few years back in their lives, were hired laborers. The prudent, penniless beginner in the world, labors for wages awhile, saves a surplus with which to buy tools or land for himself; then labors on his own account another while, and at length hires another new beginner to help him. This is the just, and generous, and prosperous system, which opens the way to all—gives hope to all, and consequent energy, and progress, and improvement of condition to all. No men living are more worthy to be trusted than those who toil up from poverty—none less inclined to take, or touch, aught which they have not honestly earned. Let them beware of surrendering a political power which they already possess, and which, if surrendered, will surely be used to close the door of advancement against such as they, and to fix new disabilities and burdens upon them, till all of liberty shall be lost.[17]

> To pressures at home and abroad were added public attacks upon Lincoln's wife. She had close relatives in the Confederate army, preferred French to British influence in the White House style, and chose to shop for her ostentatious clothing in New York or Philadelphia rather than Washington. Even Lincoln reacted bitterly to her exceeding the budget in refurbishing the White House. Her immediate predecessor had also overspent the allocation, but nobody had complained against her (Seale 1:341, 390).

14 DECEMBER 1861

"It would stink in the nostrils of the American people to have it said that the President of the United States had approved a bill overrunning an appropriation of $20,000 for flub dubs for this damned old house, when the soldiers cannot have blankets. . . . The house was furnished well enough, better than any one we ever lived in, and if I had not been overwhelmed with other business, I would not have had any of the appropriation expended, but what could I do? I could not attend to everything."[18]

> Despite being "overwhelmed," he found light diversion in the offer from the King of Siam, reminiscent of a Spanish

monarch's gift of jackasses to George Washington. The King of Siam (immortalized in the movie *The King and I*) offered a pair of elephants in English elaborately florid (Anna Leonowens, *English Governess at the Siamese Court* [Boston: Fields, Osgood, 1870], 251-52).

3 FEBRUARY 1862

This Government would not hesitate to avail itself of so generous an offer if the object were one which could be made practically useful in the present condition of the United States. Our political jurisdiction, however, does not reach a latitude so low as to favor the multiplication of the elephant, and steam on land, as well as on water, has been our best and most efficient agent of transportation in internal commerce.[19]

Loss of son Willie, 20 February, struck Lincoln deeply: "My boy is gone—he is actually gone," he said and left to solace his inconsolable wife (F2 345). He recovered more quickly, returning to work for gradual abolition in the District of Columbia along the lines he had proposed as congressman (Kurtz 250-67). But now he moved more cautiously:

24 MARCH 1862

I am a little uneasy about the abolishment of slavery in this District, not but I would be glad to see it abolished, but as to the time and manner of doing it. If some one or more of the border-states would move fast, I should greatly prefer it; but if this can not be in a reasonable time, I would like the bill to have the three main features—gradual—compensation—and vote of the people. I do not talk to members of congress on the subject, except when they ask me. I am not prepared to make any suggestion about confiscation.[20]

> A constant irritant, patronage took a heavy toll on time
> and patience as hordes sought military appointments,
> even chaplaincies. Still, Lincoln could joke about it.

May 1862

"If I have one vice, and I can call it nothing else, it is not to be able to say no! Thank God for not making me a woman, but if He had, I suppose He would have made me just as ugly as He did, and no one would ever have tempted me."[21]

> The major irritant in the course of the war continued to
> be inept generals, notoriously General George McClellan,
> who persisted in fighting a war of attrition rather than of
> aggression.

28 June 1862

Save your Army at all events. Will send re-inforcements as fast as we can. Of course they can not reach you to-day, to-morrow, or next day. I have not said you were ungenerous for saying you needed re-inforcement. I thought you were ungenerous in assuming that I did not send them as fast as I could. I feel any misfortune to you and your Army quite as keenly as you feel it yourself.[22]

28 June 1862

My view of the present condition of the War is about as follows: The evacuation of Corinth, and our delay by the flood in the Chicahominy, has enabled the enemy to concentrate too much force in Richmond for McClellan to successfully attack. In fact there soon will be no substantial rebel force any where else. But if we send all the force from here to McClellan, the enemy will, before we can know of it, send a force from Richmond and take Washington. Or, if a large part of the Western Army be brought here to McClellan, they will let us have Richmond, and retake Tennessee, Kentucky, Missouri &c. What should be done is to hold what we have in the West, open the Mississippi, and, take Chatanooga and East Tennessee, without more—a reasonable force should, in every event, be kept about Washington for it's protection. Then let the country give us a hundred thousand new troops in the shortest possible time, which added to McClellan, directly or indirectly, will take Richmond, without endangering any other place which we now hold—and will substantially end the war. I expect to maintain this contest until successful, or till I die, or am conquered, or my term expires, or Congress or the country forsakes me; and I would publicly appeal to the country for this new force, were it not that I fear a general panic and stampede would follow—so hard is it to have a thing understood as it really is.[23]

> In his role as commander-in-chief charged with extraordinary powers in wartime, Lincoln prepared a draft of the Emancipation Proclamation. Drafting portions in the telegraph office while waiting for news from the front, he showed the draft to the Cabinet on 22 July.

22 July 1862

"It had got to be midsummer, 1862. Things had gone on from bad to worse, until I felt that we had reached the end of our rope on the plan of operations we had been pursuing; that we had about played our last card, and must change our tactics or lose the game! I now determined upon the adoption of the Emancipation policy; and, without consultation with, or the knowledge of the Cabinet, I prepared the original draft of the Proclamation."[24]

SUMMER 1862

"From time to time I added or changed a line, touching it up here and there, waiting the progress of events. Well, the next news we had was of Pope's disaster, at Bull Run. Things looked darker than ever. Finally, came the week of the battle of Antietam. I determined to wait no longer. The news came, I think, on Wednesday, that the advantage was on our side. I was then staying at the Soldiers' Home. Here I finished writing the second draft of the preliminary Proclamation; came up on Saturday, called the Cabinet together to hear it, and it was published the following Monday."[25]

> This was a summer of dark discontent nationally. Republicans had lost in Fall elections, the cabinet was hopelessly split, public complaints rose loudly about threats to civil rights, abolitionists demanded immediate emancipation. General David Hunter arbitrarily freed slaves in three states, an action Lincoln revoked at once. Horace Greeley summarized the mood with an editorial, "The Prayer of Twenty Millions," on 20 August, insisting on decisive action. Lincoln replied with an open letter in the *National Intelligencer* 23 August, but one that Greeley believed had been written before his editorial had appeared (Horner 275).

23 AUGUST 1862

I have not meant to leave any one in doubt. I would save the Union. I would save it the shortest way under the Constitution. The sooner the national authority can be restored, the nearer the Union will be "the Union as it was." If there be those who would not save the Union, unless they could at the same time *save* slavery, I do not agree with them. If there be those who would not save the Union unless they could at the same time *destroy* slavery, I do not agree with them. My paramount object in this struggle *is* to save the Union, and is *not* either to save or destroy slavery. If I could save the Union without freeing *any* slave I would do it, and if I could save it by freeing *all* the slaves I would do it; and if I could save it by freeing some and leaving others alone, I would also do that. What I do about slavery, and the colored race, I do because I believe it helps to save the Union; and what I forbear, I forbear because I do *not* believe it would help to save the Union. I shall do *less* whenever I shall believe what I am doing hurts the cause, and I shall do *more* whenever I shall believe doing more will help the cause. I shall try to correct errors when shown to be errors; and I shall adopt new views so fast as they shall appear to be true views. I have here stated my purpose according to my view of *official* duty; and I intend no modification of my oft-expressed *personal* wish that all men every where could be free.[26]

> During this time of anguish at the way the war was going, Lincoln composed meditations on how man's finite mind could possibly know God's will. He allegedly said, perhaps in a moment of wishful thinking, "When the Almighty wants me to do or not to do a particular thing, He finds a way of letting me know it" (Chittenden

448). The idea of God's "willing the war" was shared by popular British orator John Bright, who thought the war was retribution for eighty years of slavery (*Speech . . . Birmingham, England* [Birmingham: J. Allen, 1862?] 19).

SEPTEMBER 1862

The will of God prevails. In great contests each party claims to act in accordance with the will of God. Both *may* be, and one *must* be wrong. God can not be *for*, and *against* the same thing at the same time. In the present civil war it is quite possible that God's purpose is something different from the purpose of either party—and yet the human instrumentalities, working just as they do, are of the best adaptation to effect His purpose. I am almost ready to say this is probably true—that God wills this contest, and wills that it shall not end yet. By his mere quiet power, on the minds of the now contestants, He could have either *saved* or *destroyed* the Union without a human contest. Yet the contest began. And having begun He could give the final victory to either side any day. Yet the contest proceeds.[27]

13 SEPTEMBER 1862

I am approached with the most opposite opinions and advice, and that by religious men, who are equally certain that they represent the Divine will. I am sure that either the one or the other class is mistaken in that belief, and perhaps in some respects both. I hope it will not be irreverent for me to say that if it is probable that God would reveal his will to others, on a point so connected with my duty, it might be supposed he would reveal it directly to me; for, unless I am more deceived in myself than I often am, it is my earnest desire to know the will of Providence in this matter. *And if I can learn what it is I will do it!* These are not, however, the days of miracles, and I suppose it will be granted that I am not to expect a direct revelation. I must study the plain physical facts of the case, ascertain what is possible and learn what appears to be wise and right. The subject is difficult, and good men do not agree.[28]

> At Secretary Seward's suggestion, Lincoln had delayed issuing the Emancipation Proclamation until Union forces achieved a major victory. McClellan's victory at Antietam justified announcing the Proclamation on 22 September.

22 SEPTEMBER 1862

"I know very well that many others might, in this matter as in others, do better than I can; and if I were satisfied that the public confidence was more fully possessed by any one of them than by me, and knew of any constitutional way in which he could be put in my place, he should have it. I would gladly yield it to him. But though I believe that I have not so much of the confidence of the people as I had some time since, I do not know that, all things considered, any other person has more; and, however this may be, there is no way in which I can have any other man put where I am. I am here. I must do the best I can and bear the responsibility of taking the course which I feel I ought to take."[29]

> Bitterly disappointed by his visit to McClellan's camp after Antietam, reportedly calling the Army of the Potomac "McClellan's body-guard," Lincoln replaced him on 5 November with General Ambrose Burnside (F2 201).

NOVEMBER 1862

"After the battle of Antietam, I went up to the field to try to get him to move and came back thinking he would move at once. But when I got home he began to argue why he ought not to move. I peremptorily ordered him to advance. It was 19 days before he put a man over the river. It was 9 days longer before he got his army across and then he stopped again, delaying on little pretexts of wanting this and that. I began to fear he was playing false—that he did not want to hurt the enemy. I saw how he could intercept the enemy on the way to Richmond. I determined to make that the test. If he let them get away I would remove him. He did so and I relieved him."[30]

> Critics within his own party, such as Carl Schurz, blamed Lincoln for Republicans' poor showing in the November elections. Schurz said the President's appointing "old democrats" resulted in the war going badly, for which the elections were "a most serious and severe reproof." In reply, Lincoln said the Republican losses came because the majority of the party were in the military; Democrats filled their vacant seats, and the press supported them (Schurz 1:216-21).

24 NOVEMBER 1862

I certainly know that if the war fails, the administration fails, and that I *will* be blamed for it, whether I deserve it or not. And I ought to be blamed, if I could do better. You think I could do better; therefore you blame me already. I think I could not do better; therefore I blame you for blaming me. I understand you *now* to be willing to accept the help of men, who are not republicans, provided they have "heart in it." Agreed. I want no others. But who is to be the judge of hearts or of "heart in it"? If I must discard my own judgment, and take yours, I must also take that of others; and by the time I should reject all I should be advised to reject, I should have none left, republicans or others—not even yourself. For, be assured, my dear Sir, there are men who have "heart in it" that think you are performing your part as poorly as you think I am performing mine. I certainly have been dissatisfied with the slowness of Buell and McClellan; but before I relieved them I had great fears I should not find successors to them, who would do better; and I am sorry to add, that I have seen little since to relieve those fears. I fear we shall at last find out that the difficulty is in our case, rather than in particular generals. I wish to disparage no one—certainly not those who sympathize with me; but I must say I need success more than I need sympathy, and that I have not seen the so much greater evidence of getting success from my sympathizers, than from those who are denounced as the contrary. It does seem to me that in the field the two classes have been very much alike, in what they have done, and what they have failed to do.[31]

> In early December, Lincoln's annual message to Congress included justifying the Emancipation Proclamation scheduled to be effective the following month. He proposed grounds more than mere expediency and, in sense and essence, anticipated the theme of the Gettysburg Address.

1 DECEMBER 1862

Is it doubted that the plan I propose, if adopted, would shorten the war, and thus lessen its expenditure of money and of blood? Is it doubted that it would restore the national authority and national prosperity, and perpetuate both indefinitely? Is it doubted that we here—Congress and Executive—can secure its adoption? Will not the good people respond to a united and earnest appeal from us? Can we, can they, by any other means so certainly or so speedily assure these vital objects? We can succeed only by concert. It is not "can *any* of us *imagine* better?" but "can we *all* do better?"

Object whatsoever is possible, still the question recurs, "can we do better?" The dogmas of the quiet past are inadequate to the stormy present. The occasion is piled high with difficulty, and we must rise with the occasion. As our case is new, so we must think anew and act anew. We must disenthrall ourselves, and then we shall save our country.

Fellow-citizens, *we* cannot escape history. We, of this Congress and this Administration, will be remembered in spite of ourselves. No personal significance, or insignificance, can spare one or another of us. The fiery trial through which we pass will light us down, in honor or dishonor, to the latest generation. We *say* we are for the Union. The world will not forget that we say this. We know how to save the Union. The world knows we do know how to save it. We—even *we here*—hold the power and bear the responsibility. In *giving* freedom to the *slave* we assure freedom to the *free*—honorable alike in what we give and what we preserve. We shall nobly save, or meanly lose, the last, best hope of earth. Other means may succeed; this could not fail. The way is plain, peaceful, generous, just—a way which, if followed, the world will forever applaud, and God must forever bless.[32]

> Amidst his troubles, Lincoln took time to compose a
> letter on the death of her father to young Fanny

136

McCullough, who suffered depression similar to that of the Lincolns upon the death of Willie the previous February.

23 December 1862

It is with deep grief that I learn of the death of your kind and brave Father; and, especially, that it is affecting your young heart beyond what is common in such cases. In this sad world of ours, sorrow comes to all; and, to the young, it comes with bitterest agony, because it take them unawares. The older have learned to ever expect it. I am anxious to afford some alleviation of your present distress. Perfect relief is not possible, except with time. You can not now realize that you will ever feel better. Is not this so? And yet it is a mistake. You are sure to be happy again. To know this, which is certainly true, will make you some less miserable now. I have had experience enough to know what I say; and you need only to believe it, to feel better at once. The memory of your dear Father, instead of an agony, will yet be a sad sweet feeling in your heart, of a purer, and holier sort than you have known before.[33]

> After standing in the New Year's reception receiving line all morning, Lincoln signed the final Emancipation Proclamation. The war went on.

1 January 1863

"I never, in my life, felt more certain that I was doing right, than I do in signing this paper. But I have been receiving calls, and shaking hands since nine o'clock this morning, till my arm is stiff and numb. Now, this signature is one that will be closely examined, and if they find my hand trembled, they will say 'he had some compunctions.' But, anyway, it is going to be done."[34]

MARCH 1863

"I am as powerless as any private citizen to shape the military plans of the Government. I have my generals and my War Department, and my subordinates are supposed to be more capable than I am to decide what movements shall or shall not be undertaken. I have once or twice attempted to act on my own convictions, and found that it was impracticable to do so. I see campaigns undertaken in which I have no faith, and have no power to prevent them; and I tell you that sometimes, when I reflect on the management of our forces, I am tempted to despair; my heart goes clear down into my boots!"[35]

> Added to attacks on his military policy, criticism of his suspending *habeas corpus* became more insistently shrill, especially after the arrest of Ohio congressman Clement Vallandigham, who was subsequently exiled to Canada. Lincoln countered with an appeal for public support in an open letter to a rally of New York Democrats with a copy to the New York *Tribune:*

12 JUNE 1863

Prior to my instalation here it had been inculcated that any State had a lawful right to secede from the national Union; and that it would be expedient to exercise the right, whenever the devotees of the doctrine should fail to elect a President to their own liking. I was elected contrary to their liking; and accordingly, so far as it was legally possible, they had taken seven states out of the Union, had seized many of the United States Forts, and had fired upon the United States' Flag, all before I was inaugerated; and, of course, before I had done any official act whatever. The present civil war soon followed; and, in certain respects, it began on very unequal terms between the parties. The insurgents had been preparing for it more than thirty years, while the government made no preparation to resist them. The former had carefully considered all the means which could be turned to their account. It undoubtedly was a well pondered reliance with them that in their own unrestricted effort to destroy Union, Constitution, and law, all together, the government would, in great degree, be restrained by the same Constitution and law, from arresting their progress. Their sympathizers pervaded all departments of the government, and nearly all communities of the people. From this material, under cover of "Liberty of speech" "Liberty of the press" and "*Habeas Corpus*" they hoped to keep on foot amongst us a most efficient corps of Spies, informers, supplyers, and aiders and abettors of their cause in a thousand ways. They knew that in times such as they were inaugerating, by the Constitution itself, the "Habeas corpus" might be suspended; but they also knew they had friends who would raise a squabble as to *who* was to suspend it; meanwhile their spies and others might remain at large to help on their cause. Or if, as has happened, the executive should suspend the writ, without ruinous waste of time, instances of arresting innocent persons might occur, as always do in such cases; and then a howl could be raised in regard to this, which might be, at least, of some service to the insurgent cause. It needed no very keen perception to discover this part of the enemies' programme, as soon as open hostilities were commenced. Yet, thoroughly imbued with a reverence for the guaranteed rights of individuals, I was slow to adopt the strong measures, which by degrees I have been forced to regard as indispensable. Nothing is better known to history than the Courts of justice are utterly incompetent to such cases. They are organized for trials of individuals, or, at most, a few individuals acting in concert; and this in quiet times, and on charges of crimes well defined in the law. Even in times of peace, bands of horse-thieves and robbers frequently grow too numerous and powerful for the courts of justice. But what comparison, in numbers, have such bands ever borne to the insurgent sympathizers even in many of the loyal states? Again, a jury can scarcely be empannelled, that will not have at least one member, more ready to hang the panel than to hang the traitor. And yet again, he who dissuades one man from volunteering weakens the Union cause as much as he who kills a union soldier in battle. Yet this dissuasion, or inducement, is no defined crime of which any civil court would take cognizance. . . . Gen. John C. Breckienridge, Gen. Robert E. Lee, Gen. Joseph E. Johnston, Gen. John B. Magruder, Gen. William B. Preston, Gen. Simon B. Buckner, and Comodore [Franklin] Buchanan, now occupying the very highest places in the rebel war service, were all within the power of the government since the rebellion began, and were nearly as well known to be traitors then as now. Unquestionably if we had seized and held them, the insurgent cause would be much weaker. But no one of them had then committed any crime defined in the law. Every one of them would have been discharged on Habeas Corpus, if the writ were allowed to operate. In view of these and similar cases, I think the time not unlikely to come when I shall be blamed for having made too few arrests rather than too many.[36]

Victory at Gettysburg, reported in the press on 7 July,

brought a crowd of serenaders to the White House where Lincoln replied with informal remarks:

7 JULY 1863

How long ago is it—eighty odd years—since on the Fourth of July for the first time in the history of the world a nation by its representatives, assembled and declared as a self-evident truth that "all men are created equal" . . . and now, in this last Fourth of July just passed, when we have a gigantic Rebellion, at the bottom of which is an effort to overthrow the principle that all men are created equal, we have the surrender of a most powerful position and army on that very day, and not only so, but in a succession of battles in Pennsylvania, near to us, through three days, so rapidly fought that they might be called one great battle on the 1st, 2d, and 3d of the month of July; and on the 4th the cohorts of those who opposed the declaration that all men are created equal, "turned tail" and run. Gentlemen, this is a glorious theme, and the occasion for a speech, but I am not prepared to make one worthy of the occasion.[37]

> Yet a week later, in a letter unsent, Lincoln bitterly chastised General George G. Meade for allowing Confederate troops to escape after their defeat at Gettysburg. "There is bad faith somewhere," he is supposed to have exclaimed, "Great God! what does it mean?" (Welles 1:370-71).

14 JULY 1863

I am very—*very*—grateful to you for the magnificient success you gave the cause of the country at Gettysburg; and I am sorry now to be the author of the slightest pain to you. But I was in such deep distress myself that I could not restrain some expression of it. I had been oppressed nearly ever since the battles at Gettysburg, by what appeared to be evidences that yourself, and Gen. Couch, and Gen. Smith, were not seeking a collision with the enemy, but were trying to get him across the river without another battle. What these evidences were, if you please, I hope to tell you at some time, when we shall both feel better. The case, summarily stated is this. You fought and beat the enemy at Gettysburg; and, of course, to say the least, his loss was as great as yours. He retreated; and you did not, as it seemed to me, pressingly pursue him; but a flood in the river detained him, till, by slow degrees, you were again upon him. You had at least twenty thousand veteran troops directly with you, and as many more raw ones within supporting distance, all in addition to those who fought with you at Gettysburg; while it was not possible that he had received a single recruit; and yet you stood and let the flood run down, bridges be built, and the enemy move away at his leisure, without attacking him. And Couch and Smith! The latter left Carlisle in time, upon all ordinary calculation, to have aided you in the last battle at Gettysburg; but he did not arrive. At the end of more than ten days, I believe twelve, under constant urging, he reached Hagerstown from Carlisle, which is not an inch over fifty-five miles, if so much. And Couch's movement was very little different.

Again, my dear general, I do not believe you appreciate the magnitude of the misfortune involved in Lee's escape. He was within your easy grasp, and to have closed upon him would, in connection with our other late successes, have ended the war. As it is, the war will be prolonged indefinitely. If you could not safely attack Lee last monday, how can you possibly do so South of the river, when you can take with you very few more than two thirds of the force you then had in hand? It would be unreasonable to expect, and I do not expect you can now effect much. Your golden opportunity is gone, and I am distressed immeasureably because of it. I beg you will not consider this a prossecution, or persecution of yourself. As you had learned that I was dissatisfied, I have thought it best to kindly tell you why.[38]

1863

"I do not know that I could have given different orders had I been with them myself; I have not fully made up my mind how I should behave, when minnie balls were whistling and these great oblong shells shrieking in my ear. I might run away."[39]

> A less serious irritant was the acknowledgment of a gift book by Shakespearean actor James Hackett in a letter that Hackett reprinted, opening the President to ridicule by literati. Lincoln dismissed his critics: "Those comments constitute a fair specimen of what has occurred to me through life. I have endured a great deal of ridicule without much malice; and have received a great deal of kindness, not quite free from ridicule. I am used to it" (*CW* 6:559).

17 August 1863

For one of my age I have seen very little of the Drama. The first presentation of Falstaff I ever saw was yours here, last winter or spring. Perhaps the best compliment I can pay is to say, as I truly can, I am very anxious to see it again. Some of Shakspeare's Plays I have never read; whilst others I have gone over perhaps as frequently as any unprofessional reader. Among the latter are Lear, Richard Third, Henry Eighth, Hamlet, and especially Macbeth. I think none equals Macbeth. It is wonderful. Unlike you gentlemen of the profession, I think the soliloquy in Hamlet commencing "O, my offense is rank," surpasses that commencing "To be or not to be." But pardon this small attempt at criticism.[40]

7

MAKING PEACE,
ALL PASSION SPENT

1863–1865

Because he was anxious about the way the war was going
in Tennessee, Lincoln did not wish to leave Washington
for a monster rally of Republicans in Springfield. He sent
a letter to an official, James C. Conkling, asking him to
read it as a speech "very slowly" so that all would understand. Instead, like the actor Hackett, Conkling printed it
to circulate even before the meeting, ensuring media
coverage but depriving the statement of dramatic imme-
diacy. The rally attracted an estimated fifty to seventy-five
thousand supporters, and the nation's press secured a
hearing that gained popular support for Lincoln's policies
at last.

26 AUGUST 1863

You dislike the emancipation proclamation; and, perhaps,
would have it retracted. You say it is unconstitutional. I
think differently. I think the Constitution invests its Com-
mander-in-Chief, with the laws of war in time of war. The
most that can be said, if so much, is that slaves are prop-

---

erty. Is there—has there ever been—any question that, by the law of war, property both of enemies and friends, may be taken when needed? And it is needed whenever taking it helps us, or hurts the enemy. Armies, the world over, destroy enemies property when they can reach it and can not use it; and even destroy their own, to keep it from the enemy. Civilized beligerants do all in their power to help themselves, or hurt the enemy, except a few things regarded as barbarous and cruel. Among the exceptions are the massacre of vanquished foes, and of non-combatants, male and female.

But the proclamation as law either is valid or is not valid. If it is not so valid, the courts will hold accordingly, and men of your views will not be hurt by it. If it is valid, it can no more be effectually retracted, than a judge can retract a judgment after its final rendering. Some of you profess to think its retraction would work favorably for the Union. Why better *after* the retraction, than *before* the issue? There was more than a year and a half of trial upon that plan before the proclamation issued, the last one hundred days of which passed under an explicit notice that the proclamation was coming unless averted by those in rebellion, returning to their allegiance. The war has certainly proceeded as favorably since its issue as before. Some generals in the field, not originally partial to the proclamation, now think it has been of service to them.

You say you will not fight to free negroes. Very well, fight exclusively to save the Union. I issued the proclamation, on purpose to aid you in the task of saving this Union. Whenever you shall have conquered all resistance to the Union, if I shall ask you to still fight on, it will then be an apt time to declare you will not fight to free negroes. I thought that, in your struggle for the Union, to whatever extent the negroes should cease helping the enemy to that extent, it weakened the enemy in their resistance to you. Do you think differently? I thought that whatever negroes can be got to do as soldiers, leaves just so much less for white soldiers to do, in saving the Union. Does it appear otherwise to you? But negroes, like other people, are creatures of motives. Why shall they do any thing for us, if we will do nothing for them? If they stake their lives for us, they must be prompted by the strongest motive—even the promise of freedom. And the promise being made, must be kept.[1]

? AUGUST 1863

Suppose those now in rebellion should say: "We cease fighting: re-establish the national authority amongst us— customs, courts, mails, land-offices—all as before the rebellion—we claiming to send members to both branches of Congress, as of yore, and to hold our slaves according to our State laws, notwithstanding anything or all things which has occurred during the rebellion." I probably should answer: "It will be difficult to justify in reason, or to maintain in fact, a war on one side, which shall have ceased on the other. You began the war, and you can end it. If questions remain, let them be solved by peaceful means—by courts and votes. This war is an appeal, by you, from the ballot to the sword; and a great object with me has been to teach the futility of such appeal—to teach that what is decided by the ballot, can not be reversed by the sword—to teach that there can be no successful appeal from a fair election but to the next election." . . . I have thus told you, once more, so far as it is for me to say, what you are fighting for. The prospects of the Union have greatly improved recently; still, let us not be over-sanguine of a speedy final triumph. Let us diligently apply the means, never doubting that a just God, in his own good time, will give us the rightful result.[2]

29 SEPTEMBER 1863

When I was a young man—long ago—before the Sons of Temperance as an organization, had an existence, I in an humble way made temperance speeches, and I think I may say that to this day I have never belied what I then said. . . . I think that the reasonable men of the world have long since agreed that intemperance is one of the greatest, if not the very greatest of all evils amongst mankind. That is not a matter of dispute, I believe. That the disease exists, and that it is a very great one, is agreed upon by all.[3]

30 SEPTEMBER 1863

"I have been in public speeches and in printed documents charged with tyranny and willfulness, with a disposition to make my own personal will supreme. I do not intend to be a tyrant. At all events, I shall take care that in my own eyes, I do not become one. I shall always try and preserve one friend within me, whoever else fails me, to tell me that I have not been a tyrant and that I have acted right."[4]

5 OCTOBER 1863

I do not feel justified to enter the broad field in regard to the political differences between radicals and conservatives. From time to time I have done and said what appeared to me proper to do and say. The public knows it all. It obliges nobody to follow me, and I trust it obliges me to follow nobody. The radicals and conservatives, each agree with me in some things, and disagree in others. I could wish both to agree with me in all things; for then they would agree with each other, and would be too strong for any foe from any quarter. They, however, choose to do otherwise, and I do not question their right. I too shall do what seems to be my duty. . . . It is my duty to hear all; but at last, I must, within my sphere, judge what to do, and what to forbear.[5]

> Speaking to a delegation from the Baltimore Synod, he reasserted publicly faith in what he called our "Common Father."

24 OCTOBER 1863

I saw before taking my position here that I was to have an administration, if it could be called such, of extraordinary difficulty, and it seems to me that it was ever present with me as an extraordinary matter that in the time of the greatest difficulty that this country had ever experienced, or was likely to experience, the man who, at the least of it, gave poor promise of ability, was brought out for duty at that time. I was early brought to the living reflection that there was nothing in the arms of this man, however there might be in others, to rely upon for such difficulties, and that without the direct assistance of the Almighty I was certain of failing. I sincerely wish that I was a more devoted man than I am. Sometimes in my difficulties I have been driven to the last resort to say God is still my only hope. It is still all the world to me.[6]

> Despite difficulties, Lincoln could find amusement in such everyday details as the courtmartial of James Madison Cutts Jr., grand-nephew of Dolley Madison and

brother of the second Mrs. Stephen A. Douglas, dismissed from the service for peeking through a hotel keyhole. This gave Lincoln the chance for an outrageous pun on the name of the Scandinavian diplomat Edward Count Piper (pronounced "peeper"), commenting that Cutts ought to have been elevated to the peerage as "Count Peeper" (Hay 76). Then he reminded Cutts of rules of self-control:

26 OCTOBER 1863

Quarrel not at all. No man resolved to make the most of himself, can spare time for personal contention. Still less can he afford to take all the consequences, including the vitiating of his temper, and the loss of self-control. Yield larger thing to which you can show no more than equal right; and yield lesser ones, though clearly your own. Better give your path to a dog, than be bitten by him in contesting the right. Even killing the dog would not cure the bite.[7]

The day after the ceremonies at Gettysburg cemetery, Lincoln replied to congratulations from Edward Everett:

20 NOVEMBER 1863

In our respective parts yesterday, you could not have been excused to make a short address, nor I a long one. I am pleased to know that, in your judgment, the little I did say was not entirely a failure. Of course I knew Mr. Everett would not fail; and yet, while the whole discourse was eminently satisfactory, and will be of great value, there were passages in it which trancended my expectation. The point made against the theory of the general government being only an agency, whose principals are the States, was new to me, and, as I think, is one of the best arguments for the national supremacy. The tribute to our noble women for their angel-ministering to the suffering soldiers, surpasses, in its way, as do the subjects of it, whatever has gone before.[8]

> Zacharia Chandler, Michigan political leader, congratulated Lincoln on Republican victories in the November elections "gloriously in every state" except New Jersey. Then he urged the President to stand firm in his annual message to Congress. Lincoln replied:

20 NOVEMBER 1863

I am very glad the elections this autumn have gone favorably and that I have not, by native depravity, or under evil influences, done anything bad enough to prevent the good result. I hope to stand firm enough to not go backward, and yet not go forward fast enough to wreck the country's cause.[9]

> In drafting the annual message, Lincoln made two telling changes in its final form: deleting the statement that emancipation had kept Europe out of the war, and revising the reference to recent elections to read "highly encouraging" rather than "not so encouraging as last year." The message concluded by warning that the war went on.

8 DECEMBER 1863

In the midst of other cares, however important, we must not lose sight of the fact that the war power is still our main reliance. To that power alone can we look, yet for a time, to give confidence to the people in the contested regions, that the insurgent power will not again overrun them. Until that confidence shall be established, little can be done anywhere for what is called reconstruction.[10]

> Among other cares, Lincoln's month-long bout with a minor case of smallpox had unnerved his wife: "I feel worried about Mary, her nerves have gone to pieces; she cannot hide from me that the strain she has been under has been too much for her mental as well as her physical health" (Helm 225).

15 DECEMBER 1863

The strongest wish I have, not already publicly expressed, is that all sincere Union men would stoutly eschew cliqueism, and, each yielding something in minor matters, all work together. Nothing is likely to be so baleful in the great work before us, as stepping aside of the main object to consider who will get the offices if a small matter shall go thus, and who else will get them, if it shall go otherwise. It is a time now for real patriots to rise above all this. As to the particulars of what I may think best to be done in any state, I have publicly stated certain points, which I have thought indispensable to the reestablishment and maintenance of the national authority; and I go no further than this because I wish to avoid both the substance and the appearance of dictation.[11]

5 FEBRUARY 1864

On principle I dislike an oath which requires a man to swear he *has* not done wrong. It rejects the Christian principle of forgiveness on terms of repentance. I think it is enough if the man does no wrong *hereafter.*[12]

7 MARCH 1864

My wish is that all who are for emancipation *in any form,* shall co-operate, all treating all respectfully, and all adopting and acting upon the major opinion, when fairly ascertained. What I have dreaded is the danger that by jealousies, rivalries, and consequent ill-blood—driving one another out of meetings and conventions—perchance from the polls—the friends of emancipation themselves may divide, and lose the measure altogether.[13]

18 MARCH 1864

In this extraordinary war extraordinary developments have manifested themselves, such as have not been seen in former wars; and amongst these manifestations nothing has been more remarkable than those fairs for the relief of suffering soldiers and their families. And the chief agents in these fairs are the women of America. I am not accustomed to the use of language of eulogy; I have never studied the art of paying compliments to women; but I must say that if all that has been said by orators and poets since the creation of the world in praise of women were applied to the women of America, it would not do them justice for their conduct during this war.[14]

22 MARCH 1864

I never knew a man who wished to be himself a slave. Consider if you know any *good* thing, that no man desires for himself.[15]

4 APRIL 1864

In telling this tale I attempt no compliment to my own sagacity. I claim not to have controlled events, but confess plainly that events have controlled me. Now, at the end of three years struggle the nation's condition is not what either party, or any man devised, or expected. God alone can claim it. Whither it is tending seems plain. If God now wills the removal of a great wrong, and wills also that we of the North as well as you of the South, shall pay fairly for our complicity in that wrong, impartial history will find therein new cause to attest and revere the justice and goodness of God.[16]

> In speaking at the Baltimore Sanitary Fair, the President omitted this portion of his draft contrasting the festivities and his passage through the city in 1861, opening by quoting Daniel Webster:

C. 18 APRIL 1864

Mr. Webster once stated the proposition that a President could not be so applauded, and ministered unto, when his term of office, and with it, his power to confer favors, drew near it's close, as he had been in the hey-day of his inaugeration. To illustrate this, he said: "Politicians—office-seekers—are not sun-flowers; they do not turn upon their god when he sets, the same look they gave when he rose." This may be a general truth; but, to my personal knowledge it is not particularly true in Baltimore. For instance, on the 22nd or 23rd of February 1861 (so near the end of one and the beginning of the other, as to be doubtful which) I passed through Baltimore, rich with honorable and fat offices, soon to be dispensed, and not one hand reached forth to greet me, not one voice broke the stillness to cheer me. Now, three years having past, and offices having passed away, Baltimore marks my coming, and cheers me when I come. Traitorous malice has sought to wrong Baltimore herein, ascribing to one cause what is justly due to another. For instance, the Richmond [*Sentinel?*] alluding to that passage through Baltimore, said: "We have no fear of any bold action by the federal government; we remember Baltimore, and our faith is unwavering in Lincoln's cowardice." Now this is hugely unjust to Baltimore. I take it to be unquestionable that what happened here three years ago, and what happens here now, was contempt of office then, and is purely appreciation of merit now.[17]

> Normally their service to the nation was acknowledged by General Orders, but troops passing through Washington would serenade the President and be rewarded with brief remarks.

22 AUGUST 1864

I almost always feel inclined, when I happen to say anything to soldiers, to impress upon them in a few brief remarks the importance of success in this contest. It is not merely for to-day, but for all time to come that we should perpetuate for our children's children this great and free government, which we have enjoyed all our lives. I beg you to remember this, not merely for my sake, but for yours. I happen temporarily to occupy this big White House. I am a living witness that any one of your children may look to come here as my father's child has. It is in order that each of you may have through this free government which we have enjoyed, an open field and a fair chance for your industry, enterprise and intelligence, that you may all have equal privileges in the race of life, with all its desirable human aspirations.[18]

> Days before the Republican national convention would meet at Chicago to nominate him against the anticipated Democratic candidate, Gen. George B. McClellan, Lincoln's pessimism deepened with rumors that even his home state of Illinois would be going Democratic. He prepared a "blind memorandum" to be signed by each member of the Cabinet without reading it:

23 AUGUST 1864

This morning, as for some days past, it seems exceedingly probable that this administration will not be re-elected. Then it will be my duty to so co-operate with the President elect, as to save the Union between the election and the inauguration; as he will have secured his election on such ground that he can not possibly save it afterwards.[19]

> Lincoln drafted a justification of his policies for a Republican rally at Buffalo where conspirators hoped to name a different standard bearer, with Horace Greeley insisting, "He cannot be elected." But Sherman's and Sheridan's military victories rallied Republicans and many Democrats to Lincoln as candidate of a fusion, Union Party. He did not send the message to Buffalo.

12 SEPTEMBER 1864

Much is being said about peace; and no man desires peace more ardently than I. Still I am yet unprepared to give up the Union for a peace which, so achieved, could not be of much duration. The preservation of our Union was *not* the sole avowed object for which the war was commenced. It was commenced for precisely the reverse object—*to destroy our Union.* The insurgents commenced it by firing upon the Star of the West, and on Fort Sumpter, and by other similar acts. It is true, however, that the administration accepted the war thus commenced, for the sole avowed object of preserving our Union; and it is not true that it has since been, or will be, prossecuted by this administration, for any other object. In declaring this, I only declare what I can know, and do know to be true, and what no other man can know to be false. In taking the various steps which have led to my present position in relation to the war, the public interest and my private interest, have been perfectly paralel, because in no other way could I serve myself so well, as by truly serving the Union. The whole field has been open to me, where to choose. No place-hunting necessity has been upon me urging me to seek a position of antaganism to some other man, irrespective of whether such position might be favorable or unfavorable to the Union. Of course I may err in judgment, but my present position in reference to the rebellion is the result of my best judgment, and according to that best judgment, it is the only position upon which any Executive can or could save the Union. Any substantial departure from it insures the success of the rebellion. An armistice—a cessation of hostilities—is the end of the struggle, and the insurgents would be in peaceable possession of all that has been struggled for. Any different policy in regard to the colored man, deprives us of his help, and this is more than we can bear. We can not spare the hundred and forty or fifty thousand now serving us as soldiers, seamen, and laborers. This is not a question of sentiment or taste, but one of physical force which may be measured and estimated as horsepower and Steam-power are measured and estimated. Keep it and you can save the Union. Throw it away, and the Union goes with it. Nor is it possible for any Administration to retain the service of these people with the express or implied understanding that upon the first convenient occasion, they are to be re-inslaved. It *can* not be; and it *ought* not to be.[20]

> Averse to campaigning for his second term, Lincoln still responded to transient troops and to delegations such as the one from Maryland celebrating their new constitution that outlawed slavery:

19 OCTOBER 1864

Something said by the Secretary of State, in his recent speech at Auburn, has been construed by some into a threat that, if I shall be beaten at the election, I will, between then and the end of my constitutional term, do what I may be able, to ruin the Government. Others regard the fact that the Chicago Convention adjourned, not *sine die,* but to meet again, if called to do so by a particular individual, as the intimation of a purpose that if the nominee shall be elected, he will at once seize control of the Government. I hope the good people will permit themselves to suffer no uneasiness on either point. I am struggling to maintain the Government, not to overthrow it. I therefore say, that if I shall live, I shall remain President until the fourth of next March; and that whoever shall be constitutionally elected therefor in November, shall be duly installed as President on the fourth of March; and that in the interval I shall do my utmost that whoever is to hold the helm for the next voyage, shall start with the best possible chance to save the ship. This is due to the people both on principle, and under the Constitution. Their will, constitutionally expressed, is the ultimate law for all. If they should deliberately resolve to have immediate peace even at the loss of their country, and their liberty, I know not the power or the right to resist them. It is their own business, and they must do as they please with their own. I believe, however, they are still resolved to preserve their country and their liberty; and in this, in office or out of it, I am resolved to stand by them.[21]

> The November election gave Lincoln 212 electoral votes
> (to McClellan's 21) and 55 percent of the popular vote.
> He easily won the soldiers' votes but only in Maryland
> were they decisive. Some estimates say that a shift of
> 80,000 votes in certain states would have given McClellan
> victory (Waugh 354; Zornow 215-16). Publicly Lincoln
> rejoiced; privately he reflected on responsibility.

8 NOVEMBER 1864

I earnestly believe that the consequences of this day's work, if it be as you assure me and as now seems probable, will be to the lasting advantage, if not to the very salvation, of the country. I cannot at this hour say what has been the result of the election; but, whatever it may be, I have no desire to modify this opinion—that all who have labored to-day in behalf of the Union organization, have wrought for the best interests of their country and the world, not only for the present, but for all future ages. I am thankful to God for this approval of the people. But while deeply grateful for this mark of their confidence in me, if I know my heart, my gratitude is free from any taint of personal triumph. I do not impugn the motives of any one opposed to me. It is no pleasure to me to triumph over any one; but

I give thanks to the Almighty for this evidence of the people's resolution to stand by free government and the rights of humanity.[22]

9 NOVEMBER 1864

"Being only mortal, after all, I should have been a little mortified if I had been beaten in this canvass before the people; but that sting would have been more than compensated by the thought that the people had notified me that all my official responsibilities were soon to be lifted off my back."[23]

10 NOVEMBER 1864

It has long been a grave question whether any government, not *too* strong for the liberties of its people, can be strong *enough* to maintain its own existence, in great emergencies.

On this point the present rebellion brought our republic to a severe test; and a presidential election occurring in regular course during the rebellion added not a little to the strain. If the loyal people, *united,* were put to the utmost of their strength by the rebellion must they not fail when *divided,* and partially paralized, by a political war among themselves?

But the election was a necessity.

We can not have free government without elections; and if the rebellion could force us to forego, or postpone a national election, it might fairly claim to have already conquered and ruined us. The strife of the election is but human-nature practically applied to the facts of the case. What has occurred in this case must ever recur in similar cases. Human-nature will not change. In any future great national trial, compared with the men of this, we shall have as weak, and as strong; as silly and as wise; as bad and good. Let us, therefore, study the incidents of this, as philosophy to learn wisdom from, and none of them as wrongs to be revenged.

But the election, along with its incidental, and undesirable strife, has done good too. It has demonstrated that a people's government can sustain a national election, in the midst of a great civil war. Until now it has not been known to the world that this was a possibility. It shows also how *sound,* and how *strong* we still are. It shows that, even among candidates of the same party, he who is most devoted to the Union, and most opposed to treason, can receive most of the people's votes. It shows also to the extent yet known, that we have more men now, than we had when the war began. Gold is good in its place; but living, brave, patriotic men, are better than gold.

But the rebellion continues; and now that the election is over, may not all, having a common interest, re-unite in a common effort, to save our common country? For my own part I have striven, and shall strive to avoid placing any obstacle in the way. So long as I have been here I have not willingly planted a thorn in any man's bosom.

While I am deeply sensible to the high compliment of a re-election; and duly grateful, as I trust, to the Almighty God for having directed my countrymen to a right conclusion, as I think, for their own good, it adds nothing to my satisfaction that any other man may be disappointed or pained by the result.

May I ask those who have not differed with me, to join with me, in this same spirit towards those who have?[24]

Those remarks to a serenade from the Lincoln-Johnson Clubs were unusual in having been scripted beforehand

161

where others had been extemporaneous. Lincoln reportedly said afterwards, "Not very graceful, but I am growing old enough not to care much for the manner of doing things." Afterward he returned to extemporaneous acknowledgments (Hay 248).

6 DECEMBER 1864

I believe I shall never be old enough to speak without embarrassment when I have anything to talk about. I have no good news to tell you, and yet I have no bad news to tell. We have talked of elections until there is nothing more to say about them. The most interesting news we now have is from Sherman. We all know where he went in at, but I can't tell where he will come out at.[25]

> For newsman Noah Brooks, Lincoln wrote out in pencil, "One speech of mine which has never been printed, and I think worth printing" as "The President's Last, Shortest, and Best Speech." He wrote it on a piece of cardboard, and so some took it as a joke (Brooks, "Personal Recollections," 230).

6 DECEMBER 1864

On thursday of last week two ladies from Tennessee came before the President asking the release of their husbands, held as prisoners of war at Johnson's Island. They were put off till friday, when they came again; and were again put off to saturday. At each of the interviews one of the ladies urged that her husband was a religious man. On saturday the President ordered the release of the prisoners, and then said to this lady "You say your husband is a religious man; tell him when you meet him, that I say I am not much of a judge of religion, but that, in my opinion, the religion that sets men to rebel and fight against their government, because, as they think, that government does not sufficiently help *some* men to eat their bread on the sweat of *other* men's faces, is not the sort of religion upon which people can get to heaven!"[26]

> On Christmas, Lincoln received a jovial despatch from General Sherman: "I beg to present you as a Christmas gift the city of Savannah with 150 heavy guns and plenty of ammunition and also about 25000 bales of cotton" (HM 32383). Lincoln replied next day:

26 December 1864

When you were about leaving Atlanta for the Atlantic coast, I was *anxious,* if not fearful; but feeling that you were the better judge, and remembering that "nothing risked, nothing gained" I did not interfere. Now, the undertaking being a success, the honor is all yours; for I believe none of us went farther than to acquiesce. . . . Not only does it afford the obvious and immediate military advantages . . . it brings those who sat in darkness, to see a great light. But what next? I suppose it will be safer if I leave Gen. Grant and yourself to decide.[27]

> Lincoln insisted on unconditional surrender. In a four-hour discussion of terms with a Confederate commission, one of them pointed out that Charles the First of England had not refused to treat with rebels. The press gave Lincoln's reply wide circulation.

3 February 1865

"I do not profess to be posted in history. On all such matters I will turn you over to Seward. All I distinctly recollect about the case of Charles I, is, that he lost his head in the end."[28]

Lincoln had the script for his second inaugural address printed, not—as with the first—for criticism but to be cut and pasted, as cue to emphases, as represented below:

4 March 1865

Fellow countrymen: At this second appearing to take the oath of the presidential office, there is less occasion for an extended address than there was at the first.

Then, a statement, somewhat in detail, of a course to be pursued, seemed fitting and proper.

Now, at the expiration of four years, during which public declarations have been constantly called forth on every point and phase of the great contest which still absorbs the attention, and engrosses the energies of the nation, little that is new could be presented.

The progress of our arms, upon which all else chiefly depends, is as well known to the public as to myself; and it is, I trust, reasonably satisfactory and encouraging to all. With high hope for the future, no prediction in regard to it is ventured.

On the occasion corresponding to this four years ago, all thoughts were anxiously directed to an impending civil war.

All dreaded it—all sought to avert it.

While the inaugural address was being delivered from this place, devoted altogether to *saving* the Union without war, insurgent agents were in the city seeking to *destroy* it without war—seeking to dissolve the Union and divide effects, by negotiation.

Both parties deprecated war; but one of them would *make* war rather than let the nation survive; and the other would *accept* war rather than let it perish.

And the war came.

One-eighth of the whole population were colored slaves, not distributed generally over the Union, but localized in the southern part of it.

These slaves constituted a peculiar, and powerful interest.

All knew that this interest was, somehow, the cause of the war.

To strengthen, perpetuate and extend this interest, was the object for which the insurgents would rend the Union, even by war; while the government claimed no right to do more, than to restrict the territorial enlargement of it.

Neither party expected for the war, the magnitude, or the duration, which it has already attained.

Neither anticipated that the *cause* of the conflict might cease with, or even before, the conflict itself should cease.

Each looked for an easier triumph, and a result less fundamental and astounding.

Both read the same Bible, and pray to the same God; and each invokes His aid against the other.

It may seem strange that any men should dare to ask a just God's assistance in wringing their bread from the sweat of other men's faces; but let us judge not, that we be not judged.

The prayers of both could not be answered—that of neither, has been answered fully.

The Almighty has His own purposes.

"Woe unto the world because of offences! for it must needs be that offences come; but woe to that man by whom the offence cometh."

If we shall suppose that American slavery is one of those offences which, in the providence of God, must needs come, but which, having continued through His appointed time, He now wills to remove; and that He gives to both north and south this terrible war as the woe due to those by whom the offence came shall we discern therein any departure from those divine attributes which the believers in a living God always ascribe to Him?

Fondly do we hope—fervently do we pray—that this mighty scourge of war may speedily pass away.

Yet, if God wills that it continue until all the wealth piled by the bondsman's two hundred and fifty years of unrequited toil shall be sunk, and until every drop of blood drawn with the lash, shall be paid by another drawn with the sword, as was said three thousand years ago, so still it must be said, "the judgments of the Lord are true and righteous altogether."

With malice toward none; with charity for all; with firmness in the right, as God gives us to see the right, let us strive on to finish the work we are in; to bind up the nation's wounds; to care for him who shall have borne the battle, and for his widow, and his orphan—to do all which may achieve and cherish a just and a lasting peace, among ourselves, and with all nations.[29]

15 MARCH 1865

Every one likes a compliment. Thank you for yours on my little notification speech, and on the recent Inaugeral Address. I expect the latter to wear as well as—perhaps better than—any thing I have produced; but I believe it is not immediately popular. Men are not flattered by being shown that there has been a difference of purpose between the Almighty and them. To deny it, however, in this case, is to deny that there is a God governing the world. It is a truth which I thought needed to be told; and as whatever of humiliation there is in it, falls most directly on myself, I thought others might afford for me to tell it.[30]

17 MARCH 1865

I was born in Kentucky, raised in Indiana, reside in Illinois, and now here, it is my duty to care equally for the good people of all the States. I am to-day glad of seeing it in the power of an Indiana regiment to present this captured flag to the good governor of their State. And yet I would not wish to compliment Indiana above other states, remembering that all have done so well. There are but few aspects of this great war on which I have not already expressed my views by speaking or writing. There is one—the recent effort of our erring brethren, sometimes so-called, to employ the slaves in their armies. The great question with them has been; "Will the negro fight for them?" They ought to know better than we; and, doubtless, do know better than we. I may incidentally remark, however, that having, in my life, heard many arguments—or strings of words meant to pass for arguments—intended to show that the negro ought to be a slave, that if he shall now really fight to keep himself a slave, it will be a far better argument why [he] should remain a slave than I have ever before heard. He, perhaps, ought to be a slave, if he desires it ardently enough to fight for it. Or, if one out of four will, for his own freedom, fight to keep the other three in slavery, he ought to be a slave for his selfish meanness. I have always thought that all men should be free; but if any should be slaves it should be first those who desire it for *themselves,* and secondly those who *desire* it for *others.* Whenever [I] hear any one arguing for slavery I feel a strong impulse to see it tried on him personally.[31]

> Plans to raise the Union flag over Fort Sumter included having the same preacher, Henry Ward Beecher, and the same general, Robert Anderson, commemorate the fall of the fort four years earlier—with added attraction of the 54th Colored Regiment. The flag would be raised at 10 A.M. but nobody was quite sure of the date, including Lincoln.

27 MARCH 1865

I feel quite confident that Sumpter fell on the thirteenth (13th) and not on the fourteenth (14th) of April. It fell on Saturday the 13th—the first call for troops on our part was got up on Sunday the 14th and given date, and issued on Monday the 15th. Look up the old Almanac and other data and see if I am not right.[32]

28 MARCH 1865

I think it is little or no difference whether the Fort-Sumpter ceremony takes place on the 13th or 14th.[33]

> From 23 March to 7 April, the President remained at Grant's headquarters, City Point, Virginia, hammering out terms of submission and visiting Richmond, but news that Secretary of State Seward had suffered a carriage accident made him anxious:

30 MARCH 1865

I begin to feel that I ought to be at home, and yet I dislke to leave without seeing nearer to the end of General Grant's present movement. He has now been out since yesterday morning, and although he has not been diverted from his programme, no considerable effect has yet been produced, so far as we know here. Last night at 10.15, when it was dark as a rainy night without a moon could be, a furious cannonade, soon joined in by a heavy musketry-fire, opened near Petersburg and lasted about two hours. The sound was very distinct here, as also were the flashes of the guns up the clouds. It seemed to me a great battle, but the older hands here scarcely noticed it, and, sure enough, this morning it was found that very little had been done.[34]

> Mrs. Lincoln had been with Tad and the President at City Point but discomfort sent her back to the White House while they remained and visited other son Robert, now a captain whose duty was to escort visitors around the camp. The Lincolns kept in touch by wire:

3 April 1865

Petersburg and Richmond are both in our hands; and Tad and I have been to the former and been with Bob four or five hours. He is well and in good spirits. Come down as you proposed.[35]

> After he had returned home and news came of Lee's surrender, a crowd estimated at three thousand followed the Quartermaster band to serenade the President in mud and rain. At his request the band played "Dixie" and followed it with "Yankee Doodle":

10 April 1865

I see you have a band of music with you. I propose closing up this interview by the band performing a particular tune which I will name. Before this is done, however, I wish to mention one or two little circumstances connected with it. I have always thought "Dixie" one of the best tunes I have ever heard. Our adversaries over the way attempted to appropriate it, but I insisted yesterday that we fairly captured it. I presented the question to the Attorney General, and he gave it as his legal opinion that it is our lawful prize. I now request the band to favor me with its performance.[36]

> Next day an insatiable crowd pressed for a longer address until, illuminated by celebrants' torches and White House lamps, the President spoke from a prepared script. He outlined plans for reconstruction, referring with praise to Louisiana's plan to confer civil rights on "the colored man"—praise that moved John Wilkes Booth to switch his own plans for the President from kidnapping to killing him. This was to be Lincoln's final public address.

11 APRIL 1865

We meet this evening, not in sorrow, but in gladness of heart. The evacuation of Petersburg and Richmond, and the surrender of the principal insurgent army, give hope of a righteous and speedy peace whose joyous expression can not be restrained. In the midst of this, however, He, from Whom all blessings flow, must not be forgotten. A call for a national thanksgiving is being prepared, and will be duly promulgated. Nor must those whose harder part gives us the cause of rejoicing, be overlooked. Their honors must not be parcelled out with others. I myself, was near the front, and had the high pleasure of transmitting much of the good news to you; but no part of the honor, for plan or execution, is mine. To Gen. Grant, his skilful officers, and brave men, all belongs. The gallant Navy stood ready, but was not in reach to take active part.

By these recent successes the re-inauguration of the national authority—reconstruction—which has had a large share of thought from the first, is pressed much more closely upon our attention. It is fraught with great difficulty. Unlike the case of a war between independent nations, there is no authorized organ for us to treat with. No one man has authority to give up the rebellion for any other man. We simply must begin with, and mould from, disorganized and discordant elements. Nor is it a small additional embarrassment that we, the loyal people, differ among ourselves as to the mode, manner, and means of reconstruction.

As a general rule, I abstain from reading the reports of attacks upon myself, wishing not to be provoked by that to which I can not properly offer an answer. In spite of this precaution, however, it comes to my knowledge that I am much censured for some supposed agency in setting up, and seeking to sustain, the new State Government of Louisiana. In this I have done just so much as, and no more than, the public knows. . . .

Some twelve thousand voters in the heretofore slave-state of Louisiana have sworn allegiance to the Union, assumed to be the rightful political power of the State, held elections, organized a State government, adopted a free-state constitution, giving the benefit of public schools equally to black and white, and empowering the Legislature to confer the elective franchise upon the colored man. Their Legislature has already voted to ratify the constitutional amendment recently passed by Congress, abolishing slavery throughout the nation. These twelve thousand persons are thus fully committed to the Union, and to perpetual freedom in the state—committed to the very things, and nearly all the things the nation wants—and they ask the nations recognition, and it's assistance to make good their committal. . . .

So great peculiarities pertain to each state; and such important and sudden changes occur in the same state; and, withal, so new and unprecedented is the whole case, that no exclusive, and inflexible plan can safely be prescribed as to details and colatterals. Such exclusive, and inflexible plan, would surely become a new entanglement. Important principles may, and must, be inflexible.

In the present "situation" as the phrase goes, it may be my duty to make some new announcement to the people of the South. I am considering, and shall not fail to act, when satisfied that action will be proper.[37]

> Among the final visitors entertained at the White House, Schuyler Colfax, Speaker of the House, was entrusted with a message to miners of the West Coast in which the President expressed unbounded optimism for national prosperity. Colfax delivered this message across the country on his trip west, as in this version delivered at Central City, Colorado.

14 APRIL 1865

"I have very large ideas of the mineral wealth of our Nation. I believe it practically inexhaustible. It abounds all over the western country, from the Rocky Mountains to the Pacific, and its development has scarcely commenced. During the war, when we were adding a couple of millions of dollars every day to our national debt, I did not care about encouraging the increase in the volume of our precious metals. We had the country to save first. But now that the rebellion is overthrown and we know pretty nearly the amount of our national debt, the more gold and silver we mine, makes the payment of that debt so much the easier. Now I am going to encourage that in every possible way. We shall have hundreds of thousands of disbanded soldiers, and many have feared that their return home in such great numbers might paralyze industry by furnishing suddenly a greater supply of labor than there will be demand for. I am going to try to attract them to the hidden wealth of our mountain ranges, where there is room enough for all. Immigration, which even the war has not stopped, will land upon our shores hundreds of thousands more per year from overcrowded Europe. I intend to point them to the gold and silver that waits for them in the West. Tell the miners from me that I shall promote their interests to the utmost of my ability; because their prosperity is the prosperity of the Nation, and we shall prove in a very few years that we are indeed the *treasury of the world.*"[38]

> That afternoon on a quiet carriage drive, the President consoled Mary Lincoln for past suffering: "We must *both,* be more cheerful in the future—between the war and the loss of our darling Willie—we have both, been very miserable" (MTL 285). And during their final moment in Ford's Theatre that evening as she leaned on his lap and looked up at him, she teased: "What will Miss Harris" (in the box with them) "think of my hanging on to you so?" Lincoln's last words were: "She won't think any thing about it" (Facs Carl Sandburg, *Lincoln Collector* [New York: Harcourt Brace, 1949], 217-18; Sandburg and Angle 226-27).

NOTES

In every instance possible the excerpts in this book derive initially from manuscript materials at either the Huntington Library or the Library of Congress. Manuscripts in the Huntington Library have prefixes and accession numbers, while those in the Lincoln papers at the Library of Congress are cited by frame number in the film supplied by the Reference Division there. These are cited when texts may differ from those in *Collected Works of Abraham Lincoln*, edited by Roy P. Basler and others, a Book-of-the-Month selection still accessible, here cited as *CW*, except for references to sketches Lincoln prepared for Jesse Fell (vol. 3) or John L. Scripps (vol. 4), abbreviated F or S, respectively, with page number. Otherwise, references to *CW* are provided even when other sources were copy texts, to offer general readers ready access to complete texts from which excerpts derived. For quotations attributed to Lincoln by others, I have applied the criteria set by Don Fehrenbacher and Virginia Fehrenbacher, *Recollected Words of Abraham Lincoln*, here abbreviated as F2. Herndon papers at the Huntington and Library of Congress, edited by Douglas Wilson and Rodney Davis as *Lincoln's Informants*, are abbreviated W&D. Among journals, the *Lincoln Herald* is abbreviated *LH*. Other abbreviations include "Facs" for facsimile, and MTL, referring to the edition of Mary Todd

Lincoln's letters, edited by Justin Turner and Linda Turner. One basic work (treated silently) for the dating is the magisterial *Lincoln Day by Day,* edited by Earl Schenck Miers and others for the Lincoln Sesquicentennial Commission.

INTRODUCTION

1. MTL 292.

1. SURVIVING THE FRONTIER

1. F 511-12.
2. To J. Lincoln, *CW* 2:217.
3. S 61.
4. To S. Lincoln, *CW* 1:456.
5. S 61.
6. To S. Haycraft, *CW* 4:70.
7. Tarbell 1:17.
8. S 61-62.
9. F 511.
10. S 62.
11. F 511.
12. *New York Tribune; CW* 4:235.
13. S 62.
14. Raymond 754.
15. Welles 2:112.
16. N. Edwards, W&D 447.
17. S 62-63.
18. *Lincoln Lore* No. 480.
19. S 63.

2. FINDING A NEW LIFE IN NEW SALEM

1. S 63.
2. *CW* 1:6.
3. S 63-64.
4. *Globe; CW* 1:510.
5. S 64.
6. Facs Sangamon Journal; *CW* 1:8-9.
7. A.Y. Ellis, W&D 171.

8. J.R. Herndon, W&D 7.
9. S 64-65.
10. Facs Rhodehamel 16; *CW* 4:121.
11. To I. Reavis, *CW* 2:327.
12. S 65.
13. Facs Harper 114; *CW* 1:48.
14. Speed 18.
15. S 65.

3. SEEKING A FORTUNE IN SPRINGFIELD

1. S 65.
2. To M. Owens, *CW* 1:78-79.
3. Ibid., 1:94-95.
4. To E. Browning, HM 25119; *CW* 1:117-19.
5. S 65.
6. *CW* 1:75.
7. S 65.
8. To J. Stuart, *CW* 1:206.
9. Unidentified transcript, HEH ms. LN2408:3:555-56.
10. To J. Stuart, Facs *LH* 45 (Oct 1943):13; *CW* 1:228.
11. Ibid., 1:229-30.
12. To. J. Speed, *CW* 1:254-58.
13. To M. Speed, *CW* 1:260.
14. To J. Speed, *CW* 2:320.
15. Ibid., 1:266.
16. Ibid., 1:280.
17. Ibid., 1:289.
18. Ibid., 1:303.
19. To E. Merryman, *CW* 1:301.
20. To S. Marshall, *CW* 1:305.
21. S 65.
22. To R. Thomas, *CW* 1:307.
23. Whig Statement, *CW* 1:315-16.
24. To J. Speed, *CW* 1:319.
25. To M. Morris, *CW* 1:320.
26. To J. Speed, *CW* 1:325.
27. F2 175-176.
28. To A. Johnston, *CW* 1:367-70, 384-85, 392; facs, Hertz 450-53.
29. To A. Johnston, *CW* 1:386-89; Basler, *Speeches,* 189-96.

4. MAKING HIS WAY WITH WIT AND WISDOM

1. To W. Durley, *CW* 1:347-48.
2. To Allen Ford, Basler, *Speeches,* 186-88; *CW* 1:382-83.
3. S 65-66.
4. To J. Speed, *CW* 1:391.
5. To W. Herndon, *CW* 1:417.
6. Ibid., 1:430-31.
7. To J. Diller, *CW* 1:444-45.
8. S 66.
9. Ottawa debate, *CW* 3:16-17.
10. To M. Lincoln, *CW* 1:465-66.
11. Ibid., 1:477.
12. S 67.
13. *Boston Advertiser,* 14 September; *CW* 2:3.
14. To C. Schlater, *CW* 2:19.
15. Howard 395.
16. Browne 1:285.
17. Patent 6469, *CW* 2:33,35.
18. To J. Addison, *CW* 2:65.
19. S 67.
20. Notes, *CW* Supplement 18-20.
21. To J. Johnston, *CW* 2:77.
22. Ibid., 2:96-97.
23. *Illinois Weekly Journal, CW* 2:124, 130.
24. Ibid., 2:136, 149-51.

5. STUMPING THE STATE AND THE NATION

1. S 67.
2. Fragment, *CW* 2:222.
3. Bloomington, Ind., speech, *CW* 2:230.
4. S 67.
5. Peoria, Ill., debate, *CW* 2:281-83.
6. To J. Scammon, *CW* Supplement 25.
7. To N. Matheny, *CW* 2:287.
8. To E. Washburne, *CW* 2:295.
9. To W. Henderson, *CW* 2:306-07.
10. To J. Speed, *CW* 2:322-23.
11. Kyle 37.
12. S 67.

13. Fragment, *CW* 2:282-83.
14. Fragment, *CW* 2:391.
15. *Illinois State Journal, CW* 2:405.
16. Fragment, *CW* 2:452-53.
17. To J. Scripps, *CW* 2:471.
18. Chicago speech, *CW* 2:489, 491, 496-97.
19. Springfield speech, *CW* 2:506.
20. Facs Rhodehamel 24; *CW* 2: 532.
21. Facs Barrett, *Immortal Letters* 78; *CW* 3:334.
22. Hay 244.
23. Facs Blair 13; *CW* 3:339.
24. To W. Ross, *CW* 3:372-73.
25. To H. Pierce, *CW* 3:375-76.
26. Facs LH 45 (1943) 8; *CW* 3:377.
27. Howells, *Lives,* 145-47; *CW* Supplement 43-44.
28. Cooper Institute speech, Tribune Tract 4, pp. 10-11; *CW* 3:550.
29. To M. Lincoln, LC exhibit (1959) 73; *CW* Supplement 49.
30. To S. Galloway, *CW* 4:34.
31. Facs Rhodehamel 33; *CW* 4:36.
32. To C. McNeill, *CW* 4:38.
33. To J. Carson, *CW* 4:39.
34. To L. Trumbull, facs Rhodehamel 33; *CW* 4:45.
35. M. Johnson, W&D 463.
36. To G. Fogg, HM 22644; *CW* 4:96.
37. To J. Babcock, *CW* 4:114.
38. To G. Bedell, facs Lorant 105; *CW* 4:129.
39. J. Nicolay, F2 340-41.
40. To G. Davis, *CW* 4:132-33.

6. Preserving, Protecting, Defending

1. Brooks, *Personal Recollections,* 224-25.
2. Nicolay and Hay, *History,* 3:248.
3. Nicolay, F2 344.
4. To G. Prentice, HM 22675; *CW* 4:184.
5. Facs Lorant 107; *CW* 4:190.
6. Lafayette, Ind., speech, *CW* 4:192.
7. *New York Tribune,* 20 February; *CW* 4: 230-31.
8. *New York Tribune,* 23 February; *CW* 4: 240-41.
9. Seward 510.
10. *New York Herald,* 1 March; *CW* 4:247.

11. J. Gillespie in R.R. Wilson 336.

12. HM 235844; *CW* 4:271; LC Film frame 7744.

13. To Congress, LC Film Frame 10514; *CW* 4:426.

14. Raymond 720.

15. To O. Browning, *CW* 4:531-32.

16. To O. Morton, HM25147; *CW* 4:541.

17. Message of the President, 18-20; *CW* 5:51-53.

18. Seale 1:390.

19. To King of Siam, *CW* 5:126.

20. To H. Greeley, *CW* 5:169.

21. Viele 818.

22. To G. McClellan, *CW* 5:289.

23. To W. Seward, *CW* 5:291-92.

24. Raymond 761.

25. Ibid., 762.

26. Facs Nicolay and Hay, *Works,* 1:326; *CW* 5:388-89.

27. Fragment, *CW* 5:403-04.

28. To Chicago clergy, *CW* 5:419-20.

29. S. Chase, F2 96.

30. Hay 232.

31. To C. Schurz, *Schurz Papers* 1:219-21; *CW* 5:509-10.

32. *Congressional Globe* 37 Cong, 3 Sess, Appendix; *CW* 5:537.

33. To F. McCullough, *CW* 5:16-17.

34. Seward, *Washington,* 2:151.

35. Winchell 37-38.

36. To New York Democrats, *CW* 6:263-65.

37. *New York Tribune,* 8 July; *CW* 5:319-20.

38. Unsent to Meade; LC Film frame 24806-08; *CW* 6:327-28.

39. Deming 41.

40. Broadside, LC Film frame 25841-43; Basler, *Speeches,* 718-19; *CW* 6:392.

7. MAKING PEACE, ALL PASSION SPENT

1. To J. Conkling, LC Film frame 25840-42; *CW* 6:408-9.

2. Fragment, *CW* 6:410.

3. To Temperance Society, *CW* 6:487.

4. W. Stoddard, F2 529.

5. To C. Drake, *CW* 5:503-04.

6. To Baltimore Synod, *CW* 6:536.

7. Draft to J. Cutts Jr., *CW* 6:538.

8. Facs Everett 16-17; *CW* 7:24-25.

9. To Z. Chandler, *CW* 7:24.

10. Draft to Congress, *CW* 7:52-53.

11. To T. Cottman, *CW* 7:66-67.

12. To E. Stanton, *CW* 7:169.

13. To J. Cresswell, *CW* 7:226.

14. D.C. Sanitary Fair, *CW* 7:254.

15. Album, HM22678; *CW* 7:260.

16. To A. Hodges, *CW* 7:282.

17. Draft Baltimore Fair, *CW* 7:303.

18. To 166th Ohio Rgt, *CW* 7:512.

19. To G. Welles, HEH ms. WE224; *CW* 7:514.

20. To I. Schermerhorn, *CW* 8:1-2.

21. To Maryland serenaders, *CW* 8:52-53.

22. To Pennsylvania serenaders, *CW* 8:96.

23. Brooks, "Personal Recollections," 226-27.

24. Facs *New York Times,* 1 February 1936; *CW* 8:100-101.

25. To serenaders, *New York Tribune,* 8 December; *CW* 8:154.

26. Brooks, "Personal Recollections," 230; *CW* 8:154-55.

27. To W.T. Sherman, *CW* 8:181-82.

28. Stephens 2:613.

29. Facs, *Upon the Occasion of the 100th Anniversary of the Second Inauguration* (Washington, D.C., 1965), 8-12.

30. To T. Weed, *CW* 8:356.

31. To 140th Indiana Rgt, *CW* 8:360-61.

32. To E. Stanton, *CW* 8:375.

33. Ibid., 376.

34. To same, O.R. 1s XLVI iii 280; *CW* 8:377-78.

35. To M. Lincoln, *CW* Supplement 285.

36. To serenaders, *CW* 8:393.

37. *New York Times,* 12 April; *CW* 8:399-405.

38. Bowles 405-6.

SELECTED BIBLIOGRAPHY

Angle, Paul M. *"Here I Have Lived."* New Brunswick: Rutgers Univ. Press, 1950.

——, ed. *Herndon's Life of Lincoln.* New York: Boni, 1936.

——, ed. *Lincoln Reader.* New Brunswick: Rutgers Univ. Press, 1947.

——. *One Hundred Years of Law.* Springfield, Ill.: Brown, Hay, Stephens, 1928.

——. *Portrait of Abraham Lincoln in Letters by His Son.* Chicago: Chicago Historical Society, 1968.

Baber, A. *A. Lincoln with Compass & Chain.* Kansas, Ill.: pvt ptd, 1968.

Barrett, Oliver. *Immortal Autograph Letters.* New York: Parke-Bernet, 1952.

——. *Lincoln's Last Speech.* Chicago: Chicago Univ. Press, 1925.

Basler, Roy, et al. eds. *Collected Works of Abraham Lincoln.* 8 vols. and supplement. New Brunswick: Rutgers Univ. Press, 1953, 1955, 1974, 1990.

——. *Abraham Lincoln: His Speeches and Writings.* Cleveland: World, 1946.

Beveridge, Albert J. *Abraham Lincoln, 1809-1858.* 2 vols. Boston: Houghton Mifflin, 1928.

Blair, Harry C. *Dr. Anson G. Henry.* Portland, Ore.?: pvt ptd., 1950.

Bowles, Samuel. *Across the Continent.* Springfield, Mass.: Bowles, 1865.

Brooks, Noah. *Abraham Lincoln.* New York: Putnams, 1909.

——. "Personal Recollections of Abraham Lincoln." *Harper's New Monthly Magazine* 31 (July 1865): 222-30.

Browne, Robert H. *Abraham Lincoln & Men of His Time*. 2 vols. Cincinnati: Jennings & Pye, 1901.

Blue, Frederic J. *Free Soilers*. Urbana: Univ. of Illinois Press, 1973.

Cunliffe, Marcus, ed. *Life of Washington*. Cambridge: Harvard Univ. Press, 1962.

Dorfman, Maurice. "Lincoln's Arithmetic Education, I." *LH* 68 (fall 1966): 61-80.

Drake, Julia. "Lincoln Land Buying." *LH* 50-51 (1948-49): 32-35.

Ellsworth, Spencer, ed. *Records of the Olden Time*. Lacon, Ill.: Home Journal, 1880.

Coleman, J. Winston. *Stage Coach Days in the Blue Grass*. Louisville: Standard, 1935.

Congressional Globe 23d-42d Congress. Washington D.C.: Globe, 1834-73.

Chittenden, L.E. *Recollections of President Lincoln*. New York: Harpers, 1891.

Deming, Henry C. *Eulogy of Abraham Lincoln*. Hartford: Clark, 1865.

Donald, David H. *Lincoln*. New York: Simon & Schuster, 1995.

Duff, John J. *A. Lincoln, Prairie Lawyer*. New York: Rinehart, 1960.

Everett, Edward. *Edward Everett at Gettysburg*. Boston: Massachusetts Historical Society, 1963.

Fehrenbacher, Don. *Prelude to Greatness*. Stanford: Stanford Univ. Press, 1962.

Fehrenbacher, Don, and Virginia Fehrenbacher. *Recollected Words of Abraham Lincoln*. Palo Alto: Stanford Univ. Press, 1996.

Harper, Robert S. *Lincoln and the Press*. New York: McGraw-Hill, 1951.

Hay, John. *Inside Lincoln's White House: Complete Civil War Diary*. Ed. Michael Burlingame and J.R.T. Ettlinger. Carbondale: Southern Illinois Univ. Press, 1997.

Helms, Katherine. *True Story of Mary, Wife of Lincoln*. New York: Harpers, 1928.

Herndon, William, and Jesse Weik. *Abraham Lincoln: the True Story of a Great Life.* 2 vols. New York: Appleton 1892.

Hertz, Emanuel. *Hidden Lincoln.* New York: Viking, 1938.

Hickey, James T. *Illinois State Historical Society Journal* 52 (1959): 202.

Horner, Harlan. *Lincoln and Greeley.* Urbana: Univ. of Illinois Press, 1953.

Howells, William Dean. *Life of Abraham Lincoln.* Springfield: Abraham Lincoln Association, 1938.

———. *Lives of Lincoln and Hamlin.* Columbus: Follet, Foster, 1860.

Howard, James Quay. "Notes on Lincoln," ed. Roy P. Basler. *Abraham Lincoln Quarterly* 4 (1947): 386-400.

Hunt, Eugenia. "My Personal Recollections of Abraham and Mary Todd Lincoln." *ALQ* 3 (March 1945): 235-52.

Jones, Edgar DeWitt. *Influence of Henry Clay upon Abraham Lincoln.* Lexington, Ky.: Henry Clay Memorial Foundation, 1952.

Jordan, Philip. "The Death of Nancy Hanks Lincoln." *Indiana Magazine of History* 40 (June 1944): 105-10.

King, Willard L. *Lincoln's Campaign Manager David Davis.* Cambridge, Mass.: Harvard Univ. Press, 1960.

Kurtz, Michael. "Emancipation in the Federal City." *Civil War History* 24 (1978): 250-67.

Kyle, Otto R. "Mr. Lincoln Steps Out." *Abraham Lincoln Quarterly* 5 (1948): 25-37.

Lamon, Ward. *Life of Abraham Lincoln.* Boston: Osgood, 1872.

Lincoln Lore. Fort Wayne, Ind.: Lincoln National Life Insurance, 1929-.

Lincoln, Abraham. *Abraham Lincoln, an Exhibition.* Washington: Library of Congress, 1959.

———. *Lincoln Day by Day.* Ed. Earl Schenck Miers, et al. 3 vols. Washington: Lincoln Sesquicentennial Commission, 1960.

———. *Message of the President.* 35th Congress. 2d Session. Washington: Globe, 1862.

———. *National Politics . . . Speech Delivered at Cooper Institute.* New York: *New York Tribune* Tract No. 4, 1860.

————. *Papers* (microfilm). Washington: Library of Congress Reference Service, 1959.

————. *Political Debates between Hon. Abraham Lincoln and Hon. Stephen A. Douglas.* Columbus: Follet, Foster, 1860.

Lincoln, Mary Todd. *Mary Todd Lincoln: Her Life and Letters.* Ed. Justin Turner and Linda Turner. New York: Knopf, 1972.

The Lincoln Way: Report of Illinois State History Library Trustees. Springfield, 1913.

Lokken, Roscoe L. *Iowa Public Land Disposal.* Iowa City: State Historical Society, 1942.

Lorant, Stefan. *Life of Abraham Lincoln.* New York: Signet, 1955.

Luthin, Reinhard. "Abraham Lincoln and the Massachusetts Whigs." *New England Quarterly* 14 (1941): 619-34.

Mearns, David C., ed. *The Lincoln Papers.* 2 vols. Garden City: Doubleday, 1948.

————. *Three Presidents and Their Books.* Urbana: Univ. of Illinois Press, 1955.

McClure, Daniel. *Two Centuries in Elizabethtown and Hardin County.* Hardin County Historical Society, 1979.

McVey, Frank. *The Gates Open Slowly.* Lexington: Univ. of Kentucky Press, 1949.

Miller, Paul L., ed. "Lincoln and the Governorship of Oregon." *Mississippi Valley Historical Review* 23 (1936): 391-94.

Nicolay, John G. *An Oral History of Abraham Lincoln.* Ed. Michael Burlingame. Carbondale: Southern Illinois Press, 1996.

Nicolay, John G., and John Hay. *Abraham Lincoln: Complete Works.* 12 vols. New York: Tandy, 1894-1905.

————. *Abraham Lincoln: A History.* 10 vols. New York: Century, 1890.

O.R.: War of the Rebellion. 128 vols. Washington: Government Printing Office, 1880-1901.

Pease, Theodore. *The Frontier State.* Chicago: McClure, 1922.

Pond, Fern Nance. *Intellectual New Salem.* Harrowgate,Tenn.: Lincoln Memorial University, 1938.

Power, John C. *Early Settlers of Sangamon County.* Springfield, Ill.: Wilson, 1876.

Pratt, Harry. *Illinois as Lincoln Knew It.* Springfield: Abraham Lincoln Associates, 1938.

———. *Personal Finances of Abraham Lincoln.* Springfield: Abraham Lincoln Association, 1943.

Randall, Ruth Painter. *Lincoln's Sons.* Boston: Little, Brown, 1955.

Rankin, Henry B. *Personal Recollections.* New York: Putnam, 1916.

Raymond, Henry J. *Life and Public Services of Abraham Lincoln.* New York: Derby and Miller, 1865.

Rhodehamel, John, and Thomas Schwartz. *"The Last Best Hope of Earth."* San Marino, Cal.: Huntington Library, 1993.

Rice, Allen Thorndike, ed. *Reminiscences of Abraham Lincoln by Distinguished Men of His Time.* New York: North American Publishing, 1886.

Rich, Wesley. *History of the U.S. Post Office to 1829.* Cambridge: Harvard Univ. Press, 1924.

Richardson, Robert Dale. *Abraham Lincoln's Autobiography.* Boston: Beacon Press, 1947.

Richmond, M.E. *Centennial History of Decatur and Macon Counties.* Decatur: Review, 1930.

Riddle, Donald W. *Congressman Abraham Lincoln.* Urbana: Univ. of Illinois Press, 1957.

———. *Lincoln Runs for Congress.* New Brunswick: Rutgers Univ. Press, 1948.

Roberts, Octavia. "We All Knew Abr'ham." *ALQ* 4 (March 1946): 17-29.

Rusk, Ralph L. *Literature of the Middle Western Frontier.* 2 vols. New York: Columbia Univ. Press, 1925.

Sandburg, Carl, and Paul M. Angle, eds. *Mary Lincoln, Wife and Widow.* New York: Harcourt, Brace, 1932.

Schurz, Carl. *Speeches, Correspondence, and Political Papers.* Ed. Frederic Bancroft. 6 vols. New York: Putnams, 1913.

Scripps, John Locke. *Life of Abraham Lincoln.* Ed. Roy Basler and L. A. Dunlap. Bloomington: Univ. of Indiana Press, 1961.

Seale, William. *The President's House.* 2 vols. Washington: White House Historical Association, 1986.

Seward, William H. *An Autobiography 1801-34.* Ed. Frederic W. Seward. New York: Appleton, 1877.

————. *Seward at Washington 1861-72.* Ed. Frederic W. Seward. New York: Derby and Miller, 1891.

Shaw, Samuel. *Journals of Major Samuel Shaw.* Edited by Josiah Quincy. Boston: Crosby and Nichols, 1847.

Simon, Paul. *Lincoln's Preparation for Greatness.* Norman: Univ. of Oklahoma Press, 1965.

Snyder, J.F. "Forgotten Statesmen of Illinois." *Transactions of Illinois State Historical Society, Number 9.* Springfield: State Historical Society, 1904.

Speed, Joshua Fry. *Reminiscences of Abraham Lincoln and Notes of a Visit to California.* Louisville: J. P. Morton, 1884.

Stephens, Alexander. *Constitutional View of the Late War.* 2 vols. Philadelphia: National Publishing, 1868-70.

Stevens, Robert. *Law School.* Chapel Hill: Univ. of North Carolina Press, 1987.

Tarbell, Ida M. *Life of Abraham Lincoln.* 2 vols. New York: Doubleday, 1900.

Thomas, Benjamin. *Abraham Lincoln.* New York: : Knopf, 1952.

————. *Lincoln's New Salem.* Springfield, Ill.: Abraham Lincoln Association, 1934.

Thompson, Charles M. "Illinois Whigs before 1846." *University of Illinois Studies in Social Science* 4 (1915).

Venable, W.H. *Beginning of Literary Culture in the Ohio Valley.* Cincinnati: Clarke, 1891.

Viele, Egbert. "A Trip With Lincoln, Chase, and Stanton," *Scribner's Monthly* 16 (October 1878): 813-22.

Volk, L.W. "The Lincoln Life-Mask and How It Was Made." *Century* 23 (December 1881): 223-28.

Ward, William H. *Abraham Lincoln: Tributes from His Associates.* New York: Crowell, 1895.

Warren, Louis B. *Lincoln's Youth.* Indianapolis: Indiana Historical Society, 1959.

Waugh, John C. *Reelecting Lincoln, the Battle for the 1864 Presidency.* New York: Crown, 1997.

Weik, Jesse W. *The Real Lincoln.* Boston: Houghton Mifflin, 1922

Welles, Gideon. *Diary*. Ed. H.F. Beale and A.W. Brownsword. New York: Norton, 1960.

Whitney, Ellen M., ed. *The Black Hawk War*. 2 vols. Springfield: Illinois State Historical Library, 1970.

Wiley, Earl W. *Four Speeches by Abraham Lincoln*. Columbus: Ohio State Univ. Press, 1927.

Wilson, Douglas L. *Honor's Voice*. New York: Knopf, 1998.

———. *Lincoln before Washington*. Urbana: Univ. of Illinois Press, 1997.

———. "That Fatal First of January." *Civil War History* 38 (1992): 101-30.

Wilson, Douglas, and Rodney Davis. *Herndon's Informants*. Urbana: Univ. of Illinois Press, 1998.

Wilson, Rufus R., ed. *Intimate Memories of Lincoln*. Elmira: Primavera, 1945.

Winchell, John M. "Three Interviews with President Lincoln." *Galaxy 16* (July 1873): 33-41.

Zall, P.M. *Abe Lincoln Laughing*. Knoxville: Univ. of Tennessee Press, 1997.

Zornow, William. *Lincoln and the Party Divided*. Westport: Greenwood, 1954.

INDEX

Index

Index

Dilworth, Thomas, *Schoolmaster's Assistant*, 12
District of Columbia, 35; slavery in, 44, 79-80, 127-28. *See also* Washington, D.C.
"Dixie" (D.D. Emmitt), 169
Doctrine of Necessity, 71
dogmas, 136
Don Quixote (M. Cervantes), 87
Dorsey, Azel W., 12
Douglas, Adele Cutts (Mrs. S.A.), 150
Douglas, Stephen A.: and A.L., 28, 87-88, 91-93, 95-99, 101; campaigns 1858, 101; campaigns 1860, 113; debates, 102-04; and Missouri Compromise, 88; prevails, 122
Dred Scott decision, 97
duel, A.L.'s, 54-55. 58
Dummer, Henry E., 30

economics: capital, 106, 125; commerce, 127; labor, 105-6, 125;
  right to rise, 105-07, 125-26, 155-56; war debt, 172-73
education: Kentucky, 8, 30; Indiana, 12; Illinois, 12-14; legal, 31-34
Edwards, Ninian, 36, 55
elections, wartime, 160. *See also* campaigns
elephant, 127
Elizabethtown, Ky., 11
Ellis, Abner Y., 26
emancipation, 86, 130, 153. *See also* abolition
Emancipation Proclamation, 129-30, 133, 135, 137-38; effects of, 135, 145-47, 157-58

Erie, Penn., 112
Episcopal church, 58
Everett, Edward, letter to, 150-51

Falstaff, Sir John (Shakespeare), 143
Faulkner, William, 64
financial affairs, A.L.'s, 15-16, 21, 24; barter, 30; honoraria, 109; 1840 income, 59; "national debt," 28-29; wages, 29, 58, 105
flatboating, 15-16, 21-22, 58, 81
Ford's theatre, 173
Fort Sumter, 116, 157, 168
founding fathers, 13, 119-20
free elections, 160. 171
Free Soil party, 79
Fremont, Gen. John C., 96, 124

Gaines, John Pollard, 81
generals, field, 146
Gentry, Allen, 16
Gentry, Matthew, 60
Gettysburg address, 135, 150
Gettysburg, battle of, 140, 142
Gettysburg cemetery, 150
Globe tavern (boarding house), 58
God, 33, 71, 170; aid of, 100-101, 117, 159-61; governance, 105-6, 128, 148-49, 167; will of, 106, 131, 154, 165-66. *See also* religion
Gold, 161, 173
Gott, Daniel, 80
Government (U.S.), 106-07, 116, 123, 127, 155-56
Grant, Gen. Ulysses S., 163, 168, 170
Greeley, Horace, 107, 130, 156; letter to, 131

Index

Index

Index

Swaney (Sweeney), James, 12
Taylor, Zachary, 72, 81
temperance, 104, 148
Tennessee, 129, 145, 162
Texas, annexation of, 69, 74, 80
Thirteenth Amendment, 171
Thomas, Richard, Jr., letter to, 56
Todd, Robert S. (father-in-law), 84
Trailor "murder" case, 47-51
Transylvania University, 30, 81
tremetol poisoning ("milk sick"), 11, 17
Trumbull, Lyman, 93
turkeys, 11
tyranny, A.L. accused of, 148

Union, the: as U.S.A., 100, 115, 118, 122, 131, 136, 171; in politics, 107, 152; threats to, 107, 138-40, 146, 157
Union party, 156, 159, 161
Vallandigham, Clement L., 138
Vandalia, Ill., 32, 43
Virginia, 7
Volk, Leonard, 111

War Department, 138
war powers, 145, 157-58
Washington, D.C., 126, 145; as capital, 93, 121, 129, 155; trip to, 112, 118-21. *See also* District of Columbia, White House
Washington, George, 97-98, 107, 127
Webster, Daniel, quoted, 97, 154
Weems, Mason L. (*Life of Washington*), 13
Whig, A.L. as, 25, 75, 77
Whig party: in Illinois, 30, 35, 56-58, 69; national, 58, 73, 79, 93
White House, 126, 141, 155, 169-70
"Wide Awake" clubs, 112
Wisconsin, 24
women: A.L. and, 33, 37, 88, 128, 162; praise of, 151, 153
wrestling, 101
Wythe, George, 86

"Yankee Doodle," 169
Yates, Richard, 89